John Newton and George Whi
as leaders of the eighteenth-cent
now, however, no one has done th
show how much they knew abou
each other, and communicated ea¡   .. Grant
Gordon's careful research has uncov....u an important story, both
for fleshing out the early history of modern evangelicalism and
offering an encouraging picture of that evangelicalism at its best.

Mark A. Noll

Author of *From Every Tribe and Nation: A Historian's Discovery of the Global*
Christian Story
Francis A. McAnaney Professor of History
University of Notre Dame, Indiana

God did some amazing things in the eighteenth century in the
trans-Atlantic revival, and some of that was done in the life
of the author of *Amazing Grace*, John Newton. In this engaging
book, Grant Gordon traces the life and ministry of Newton
with a special focus on the ways in which his life intersected
with the even more famous George Whitefield. The book gave
me fresh insights into the ministries of those special men, and
a fresh appreciation for the grace of God that enabled them.
This is history worth reading and pondering.

Stanley K. Fowler

Author of *More Than a Symbol: The British Baptist Recovery of Baptismal*
Sacramentalism
Professor of Theological Studies
Heritage College & Seminary
Cambridge, Ontario

George Whitefield and John Newton were two of the titans of
eighteenth-century British evangelicalism. But for too long, the
precise nature of their mutual influence has remained unclear.
Grant Gordon's much-needed book rectifies that problem
with its treasure trove of illuminating research.

Thomas S. Kidd

Author of *George Whitefield: America's Spiritual Founding Father*
Distinguished Professor of History, Baylor University
Waco, Texas

This is a spiritually delightful and historically valuable study of the precious relational dynamic between two of the greatest Anglican evangelicals of the eighteenth century. It is a real joy to grasp how such noble souls can urge one another on in God's service and be a tremendous power for good across the land and across the centuries. Grant Gordon is master of the intimate details, connections and comparisons, and has done us a great service, showing how one faithful minister can be such a positive spiritual and personal influence on another. I heartily commend it and pray it will be both a spur and a blessing to many.

Lee Gatiss
Director of Church Society (www.churchsociety.org)
and Editor of *The Sermons of George Whitefield*
Cambridge, England

This is a beautifully written book which brings Whitefield and Newton alive for a new generation. Grant Gordon is an excellent scholar whose work is carefully researched and accurate. His book also has the merit of being highly readable. This is a work of serious history which is also a page turner. There is much here to inform the mind and challenge the heart. Warmly recommended.

Peter J. Morden
Author of *The Life and Thought of Andrew Fuller, 1754-1815*
Vice Principal, Spurgeon's College, London

George Whitefield was the greatest preacher of the Evangelical Revival and John Newton the ablest exponent of its pastoral psychology. They shared the conviction that the truths of vital Christianity transcend denominational loyalties and so inspired many from a variety of backgrounds to discover and advance in the spiritual life. Grant Gordon has written a full and careful study of their relations which reveals something of the calibre of the two men as devoted Christian leaders.

David William Bebbington
Author of *The Dominance of Evangelicalism: The Age of Spurgeon and Moody*
Professor of History, University of Stirling
Stirling, Scotland

Dr. Gordon has made an invaluable contribution to new understanding of the shared theology and history of these two great servants of the Lord.

How Whitefield led Newton, to gain a stronger faith, and the skills of an outstanding fellow preacher of the Gospel, is an inspiring story. I could not recommend it more.

Jonathan Aitken
Author of *John Newton: From Grace to Amazing Grace*
Former Politician and well-respected biographer
London

A Great Blessing to Me

John Newton Encounters
George Whitefield

GRANT GORDON

Dr. Grant Gordon has graduate degrees from both Gordon-Conwell Theological Seminary and Princeton Theological Seminary. For eighteen years he served as pastor in Baptist churches on Ontario, Canada. Following this he was Director of Supervised Ministry and lecturer in Baptist History at Tyndale Theological Seminary, Toronto. Afterwards he served as Transitional Pastor in numerous short-term assignments. Now retired, he and his wife Margaret live in Stouffville, Ontario. He continues to do extensive research and writing about the 18th century church, especially in the U.K. He is editor of *Wise Counsel: John Newton's Letters to John Ryland Jr.*

Copyright © Grant Gordon 2016

paperback ISBN 978-1-78191-715-2
epub ISBN 978-1-78191-731-2
Mobi ISBN 978-1-78191-732-9

10 9 8 7 6 5 4 3 2 1

Published in 2016
by
Christian Focus Publications,
Geanies House, Fearn, Ross-shire,
IV20 1TW, Scotland, Great Britain.

www.christianfocus.com

Cover design by
Moose77

Printed and bound by
Bell and Bain, Glasgow

MIX
Paper from
responsible sources
FSC® C007785
www.fsc.org

John Newton portrait, p. 16, Church Mission Society

CONTENTS

Foreword

Two of the most remarkable figures of the eighteenth century and both together in this excellent study of a segment of their lives: who could ask for a better read! George Whitefield, regarded as the preaching wonder of his day, and John Newton, one of the leading spiritual guides of the movement that Whitefield had a significant hand in creating, Evangelicalism, are perennially interesting figures. Whitefield's winsomeness, his transparency of heart, and his devotion to Christ are deeply encouraging in our day of glittering image and little substance when Christ's name and message are trashed (though the latter was true in Whitefield's day as well). And Newton, equally winsome, refreshingly catholic in his embrace of all who truly loved the Lord Jesus, and a truly wise man, is also a tonic in our day of division—ironic since we have the social media that theoretically should help overcome such divisions. These lives, intertwined as this study of a portion of those lives reveals, speak across the centuries to our day. History matters in its own right, and it should not be distorted to fit modern agendas (a great tendency in our illiberal day when people take offence at anything but their own views). On the other hand, one reason for the study of the past is to learn wisdom for the present. And these two marvelous characters have much to teach contemporary Christians. To top it off, Dr. Gordon has a wonderful gift for detailed analysis and for displaying the broader historical context and contours, and then pointing out the take-away lessons from the past. So this turns out to be a great read for both the professional historian and the thoughtful Christian.

Michael A.G. Haykin
Southern Baptist Theological Seminary
Louisville, Kentucky, U.S.A.
July 2015.

Acknowledgments

Special thanks to the following libraries and archives for permission to quote material in their holdings: Bridwell Library Special Collections (Southern Methodist University), David M. Rubenstein Rare Book & Manuscript Library (Duke University), Dr. Williams Library (London), Firestone Library (Princeton University), Lambeth Palace (London), The Morgan Library and Museum (New York), Seattle Pacific University Library (Seattle, Wash.), Thomas Fisher Rare Book Library (University of Toronto), and West Yorkshire Archive Service (West Yorkshire).

Thanks to my friends Marylynn Rouse for sharing some Newton material, Michael Haykin for his encouragement in this writing project and Linda Leggett for proofreading the first draft. Thanks to the staff of Tyndale University-College Library, Toronto, and for inter-library loan service.

I express my appreciation to Christian Focus Publications for their interest in publishing this book and for the work of Anne Norrie and Kate MacKenzie in preparing it for publication.

I express my gratitude to my wife Margaret for her encouragement and patience, as well as reading my various instalments and providing feedback during the final phase of this book. I dedicate this book to her.

Abbreviations and Symbols

*	A single asterisk indicates spelling in the original.
[ ]	Material or comments in square brackets have been added by the editor.
Aitken, *Newton*	Jonathan Aitken, *John Newton: From Disgrace to Amazing Grace* (Wheaton, 2007).
An Authentic Narrative	*An Authentic Narrative of Some Remarkable and Interesting Particulars in the Life of ***** Communicated in a Series of Letters the Rev. Mr. Haweis, Rector of Aldwincle, Northamptonshire and by Him (at the request of Friends) Now Made Public* (1764). This has been published under various names. Reprinted in Bruce Hindmarsh, *The Life and Spirituality of John Newton* (Vancouver, 1998), 11-95. The pagination is from this work.
Bull, *Newton*	Bull, Josiah, *Now I See: The Life of John Newton* (Edinburgh reprint, 1998). First published as *John Newton of Olney and St. Mary Woolnoth* (1868).
Cecil/Rouse, *Newton*	Richard Cecil; ed. Marylynn Rouse, *The Life of John Newton* (Christian Focus Publications, Fearn, Ross-shire, 2000).
Dallimore, *Whitefield*, 1, 2	*George Whitefield*, 2 vols. (Edinburgh; American Edition 1980).
Dallimore, *Whitefield*	Dallimore, Arnold, *George Whitefield: God's Anointed Servant in the Great Revival of the Eighteenth Century* (Westchester, Ill., 1990).

DEB	D. M. Lewis, ed., *Dictionary of Evangelical Biography, 1730–1860*, 2 vols. (Oxford, 1995; Peabody, Mass., reprint, 2004).
Diary [1]	Newton diary (22 Dec. 1751-5 June 1756) in Firestone Library, Princeton University.
Diary [2]	Newton diary (23 Sept. 1756- 31 Dec. 1773), in The Morgan Museum and Library, New York.
Diary [3]	Newton diary (1 Jan. 1773-21 Mar. 1805) in Firestone Library, Princeton University.
Diary [1767]	Newton diary (1 Jan. 1767-31 Dec. 1767) in Lambeth Palace, London.
Gillies, *Whitefield*	John Gillies, *Memoirs of the Life of the Rev. George Whitefield* (London, 1772).
Gillies, *Whitefield Works*	John Gillies, *The Works of the Reverend George Whitefield* (London, 1771-1772).
Gordon, *Wise Counsel*	Grant Gordon, ed., *Wise Counsel: The Letters of John Newton to John Ryland Jr.* (Edinburgh, 2009).
Hindmarsh, *Newton*	Bruce Hindmarsh, *John Newton and the English Evangelical Tradition* (Oxford, 1996).
Johnston, *Whitefield*	E. A. Johnston, *George Whitefield: A Definitive Biography*, 2 vols. (Stoke-on-Trent, 2008).
Newton (Clunie)	John Newton, *The Christian Correspondent; or a series of religious letters, written by John Newton ....to Alex. Clunie* (Hull, 1790).
ODNB	Oxford Dictionary of National Biography (1994; also online edition, 2010).
Philip, *Whitefield*	Robert Philip, *The Life and Times of George Whitefield* (1837; Edinburgh reprint, 2009).
Tyerman, *Whitefield*	Luke Tyerman, *The Life of the Rev. George Whitefield*, 2 vols. (New York, 1877).
Works	John Newton, *The Works of John Newton*, 6 vols. (1820, Edinburgh reprint, 1985).

Introduction

This book was to be a study of the relation between John Newton (1725-1807) and the two great eighteenth century evangelists, John Wesley (1703-1791) and George Whitefield (1714-1770). But as work progressed it seemed best to publish two separate volumes so that each evangelist could have the attention he deserved. This volume focuses on the relation between Newton and Whitefield, whom Newton met first. Hence, much that relates to John Wesley will be set aside until the second volume.

Sadly today the great English evangelist George Whitefield is not as well known as he deserves to be. Equally unfortunate is that many are unaware of significant details of John Newton's life; other than that he was a former slave-ship captain who became a minister and who wrote the hymn *Amazing Grace*. Further, it will come as a surprise to almost all to learn that Whitefield had a fifteen-year friendship with Newton.

Whitefield's biographers have largely overlooked their connection. John Gillies, who in 1772 was Whitefield's first biographer, includes an excerpt of the sermon Newton preached upon Whitefield's death, but mentions nothing more.[1] Whitefield's early biographies by

---

1. Gillies, *Whitefield*, 341-346.

Tyerman (1877, 78) and Philip (1833) mention that Newton admired Whitefield but give little, if any details.[2] Dallimore, in his monumental two-volume biography that drew fresh attention to Whitefield in 1970s, quotes two brief portions of Newton's sermon at Whitefield's death but devotes only a short paragraph to him.[3] Four more recent major studies of Whitefield (probably because of the focus of their study) do not mention Newton at all.[4]

Many of Newton's biographers mention Whitefield, but most give little detail. Josiah Bull, in 1868, was the first Newton biographer to quote from Newton's manuscript diaries and letters. These were passed down to him from his grandfather (Rev. William Bull) who was Newton's personal friend.[5] Drawing from these documents, he fleetingly mentions Whitefield. Bruce Hindmarsh's landmark book *John Newton and the Evangelical Secession* (1996) rekindled attention on Newton, especially on two of these diaries (now at Princeton University). He nicely, though

---

2. Tyerman, *Whitefield*, 2:624, 625; Philip, *Whitefield*, 511 (who mentions only that Newton preached a sermon in honour of Whitefield).

3. Dallimore, *Whitefield*, 2:291, 531, 533.

4. Thomas S. Kidd, *George Whitefield: America's Spiritual Founding Father* (New Haven, Conn., 2014); Jerome Dean Mahaffey, *The Accidental Revolutionary: George Whitefield & the Creation of America* (Waco, Tex., 2011), Frank Lambert, *'Pedlar in Divinity': George Whitefield and the Transatlantic Revivals* (Princeton, N.J., 1994); Harry S. Stout, *The Divine Dramatist: George Whitefield and the Rise of Modern Evangelicalism* (Grand Rapids, Mich., 1991).

5. Bull, *Newton* (1868). In his references to Whitefield, Donald Demaray, *The Innovation of John Newton* (Lewiston, N.Y., 1988) draws from only previously published material, especially Bull.

briefly, summarises Whitefield's influence on Newton.[6] Since then, other Newton biographers have mentioned Whitefield, though references have often been in bits and pieces.[7]

Newton's relationship with Whitefield deserves to be told in detail, drawing from all known resources. In addition to the two manuscript Newton diaries at Princeton University, the following study will include a third manuscript Newton diary and other letters not available to biographers since 1868, and some not known at all. By including a full transcript of key sections of Newton's diaries we are able to let him speak for himself so that we can see and hear Whitefield through Newton's eyes and ears.

We will also include all known correspondence between them. In particular we will take notice of how Whitefield (directly and indirectly) influenced Newton on his quest for greater understanding of his faith and for clearer direction in his life. In the process, this study will provide an overview of both of their lives. First we will review their lives before their paths crossed.

---

6. Hindmarsh, *Newton*, 72-74. Bernard Martin, in *An Ancient Mariner: A Biography of John Newton* (London, 1950) drew from this MS two volume diary when it was housed in England, before it was deposited in Princeton University. But because he used no footnotes it is most difficult to trace his sources. Martin acknowledged that his book was "most un-scholarly" (Martin to Professor N. C. Hannay, 26 Jan. 1951). Copy of letter in possession of author.

7. Marylynn Rouse in her edited and much expanded reprint of Richard Cecil, *Life of John Newton* (1827; reprint, Christian Focus Publications, Fearn, Ross-shire, 2000), see 90- 94 (hereafter Cecil/Rouse, *Newton*); William E. Phipps, *Amazing Grace in John Newton: Slave Ship Captain, Hymn Writer and Abolitionist* (Macon, Ga., 2001); Aitken, *Newton*.

John Newton, aged sixty-three

Pastel drawing by John Russell RA, in 1788, when Newton was not only a popular pastor and revered writer of spiritual letters, but was in the midst of his campaign against the slave trade. This portrait now hangs in the head office of the Church Mission Society in Oxford to honour him as one of the founders of the CMS in 1799.

1

The Lives of John Newton and George Whitefield till mid-1750s

John Newton

John Newton was born 24 July 1725 in Wapping, East London, to a pious Congregationalist mother who taught him Isaac Watts' hymns and the *Westminster Shorter Catechism*. But she died when Newton was six and his father, a sea captain, soon remarried. When John was eleven, he joined his father at sea and over the next six years made five voyages to the Mediterranean. At seventeen, he visited family friends near London where he met and immediately fell in love with thirteen-year-old Mary Catlett. On one of his later excursions to see her, he was press-ganged and forced into royal naval service on the *H.M.S Harwich*. Soon after he deserted but was caught, brought back to the ship and 'kept a while in irons ... publicly stripped,'[1] whipped and demoted. The ship set sail for the East Indies,[2] a journey that was to last five years. On the way the fleet anchored for supplies at Madeira, an Atlantic island off the coast of Portugal. The day before continuing their journey, he was abruptly awakened from his sleep below the deck to learn that his captain was

---

1. Richard Cecil, *Memoirs of the Rev. John Newton*, in *Works*, 1:10.
2. This refers to the many islands off the SE coast of Asia, including Sumatra, Java, Borneo, New Guinea and the Philippines.

about to exchange two of his crew for two from another ship nearby. This was his chance to get off his ship so he could return sooner to see Mary. Further, he had been in constant conflict with the captain. So he pled to be exchanged. The captain agreed and within a few minutes he was aboard a new vessel and thrilled he had also escaped the long journey to the East Indies. But he had boarded not just any ship, but a Guinea ship – a Slave ship. He was only nineteen and little did he know that his time in the slave trade would last nine long years and that he would experience things that would shape and change his life forever. [3]

For six months they bought slaves along the west coast of Africa. Then just as the ship was set to sail for the 'middle passage' of the trans-Atlantic slave trade, he opted to go ashore at Sierra Leone. There he worked in the trade, 'purchasing and collecting slaves, to sell to the vessels that arrived from Europe.'[4] As things went from bad to worse caused by illness, mistreatment by his employer's African mistress who treated him almost as a slave, and his own stubbornness, he sank lower in Africa. Of this time, he commented much later, 'I entered into closer engagements with the inhabitants, and should have lived and died a wretch amongst them, if the Lord had not watched over me for good.'[5] He would never forget that experience. During this time his father tried to find him and asked his friend Joseph Manesty of Liverpool to have his African-bound ships look out for him. Providentially,

---

3. The first paragraphs are adapted from Gordon, *Wise Counsel*, 1-4.

4. Newton, *Thoughts upon the African Slave Trade*, in *Works* 6:522.

5. Letter 6, *An Authentic Narrative*, 46.

he was found by the *Greyhound* that was dealing in gold, ivory and beeswax. Newton said, 'Had the ship passed one quarter of an hour sooner, I would have died there a wretch, as I had lived.'[6] He came aboard and after the ship had loaded enough cargo along the coast, they sailed for home.

But in the Atlantic between the coast of Newfoundland and Ireland they hit a violent storm. The relentless waves hammered the ship as the crew frantically pumped water and did everything they could to survive. When it appeared the ship was going to sink, Newton, who was exhausted from manning the pumps and steering at the helm, thought he was doomed. So he cried out to God for help and mercy. That moment on 10 March 1748 was the beginning of his new birth. Of this, he later said,

> I ... was ... sincerely touched with a sense of the undeserved mercy I had received, in being brought safe through so many dangers. I was sorry for my past misspent life, and purposed an immediate reformation. ... to all appearance, I was a new man.... I acknowledged the Lord's mercy in pardoning what was past, but depended chiefly upon my own resolution to do better for the time to come. I had no Christian friend or faithful minister to advise me that my strength was no more than my righteousness... Therefore I consider this as the beginning of my return to God, or rather of his return to me; but I cannot consider myself to have been a believer (in the full sense of the word) till a considerable time afterwards.[7]

---

6. Newton, quoted in Cecil, *Memoirs of Newton* in *Works*, 1:46.
7. Newton, quoted in Cecil, *Memoirs of Newton* in *Works*, 1:32, 33.

That was the turning point for him and afterwards on each anniversary of that day[8] he would spend in quiet meditation and reflection. 'He was not yet a "true believer": that came six months later.'[9] Fortunately the storm gradually subsided, and the broken ship limped onward and landed in Ireland for repairs. When he arrived back at Liverpool, Newton was offered a slave vessel of his own by his father's friend Manesty. Instead he asked to serve as first-mate (next in command to the captain) to gain more experience, before becoming a captain. He was not yet twenty-three.

In all, Newton would lead four slaving voyages; one as a first-mate on the *Brownlow* carrying slaves to Charleston, and three as captain of his own ship, taking slaves to the West Indies. When he became a captain, he tried to follow his new-found Christian ideals and wrote in his diary; 'I will treat them with humanity while under my power and not render their confinement grievous.'[10] In 1764 (ten years after leaving the trade), in his autobiography, *An Authentic Narrative*, he admitted that while in the slave trade he 'never had the least scruple as to its lawfulness.' But even at that time, he admitted to being 'shocked' and said he felt like a jailer who was 'perpetually conversant with chains, bolts and shackles.' Hence he had 'often prayed' that God would provide a more

---

8. After the change to the Gregorian calendar in 1752, John adjusted his date accordingly by eleven days and celebrated it on 21 March.

9. Bruce Hindmarsh, 'Newton, John (1725-1807)', *ODNB*, Oxford University Press, 2004 <http://www.oxforddnb.com/view/article/20062>[accessed 20 Jan 2014].

10. Quoted in Steve Turner, *Amazing Grace* (New York, N.Y., 2002), 61.

'humane calling.' He also wanted to 'have more fellow-ship with his [God's] people and ordinances' and be freed from 'long separations from home.'[11] In 1793, almost forty years after he had quit the trade he wrote, 'I ... thought myself bound to treat the slaves under my care with gentleness, and so consult their ease and convenience, as far as was consistent with the safety of the whole family of whites and blacks on board my ship.'[12]

After his successful voyage as first-mate on the *Brown-low*, and with Manesty's promise to provide him a ship of his own, Newton proposed to Mary Catlett, whom he often affectionately called Polly. In February 1750 they were married near the Catlett home in Chatham. But in August, soon after his twenty-fifth birthday, he sailed as ship captain and was away from her for long stretches of time during his next three voyages.

Because of his voyages, he was far removed from Christian counsel. Therefore, that year (1750) as he was about to set sail he began a correspondence with Dr. David Jennings (1691-1762), the Congregational pastor of Newton's mother in Wapping, where he spent his early childhood.[13] After introducing himself by mentioning his mother, he asked permission to write occasionally. The purpose: 'to beg your guidance and advice to conduct me through the busy world I am just entering upon' and 'direction on

---

11. The previous quotes are all from Letter 13, *An Authentic Narrative*, 88.

12. See Newton's footnote that he added in 1793 in *Letters to a Wife* in *Works*, 5:407. See a similar comment in *Thoughts upon the African Slave Trade* in *Works*, 6:523.

13. Here I am following Hindmarsh, *Newton*, 67, 68.

difficult points.'[14] Understandably, pastor Jennings was happy to water the seed that he and Newton's mother had planted in John when he was a little boy. Consequently Jennings, who was a firm Calvinist, guided Newton in that direction of doctrine, acted as his spiritual adviser, and responded to his questions. They would correspond till Jennings' death in 1762.

During this time, Newton lamented two concerns: 'As to preaching, I heard none but of the common sort, and had hardly an idea of any better' and second, 'neither had I the advantage of Christian acquaintance.'[15] On the high seas he had not met a strong Christian seafaring person, especially at his rank, so he said he felt 'like Elijah' who thought he was alone in following God.[16] But this dramatically changed when, on what would be his final voyage home, he docked June 1754 at St. Christopher (St. Kitts) in the West Indies. There in the harbour he met Alexander Clunie who was a vibrant Christian from London and was like Newton, a captain of a ship (though carrying cargo, not slaves)[17]. Before meeting Clunie he said, 'my conceptions were, in many respects, confused: not having,

---

14. Newton to Jennings, 6 July 1750, MS #39.98(46) in Dr. Williams Library, London. This library has thirteen MS letters of Newton to Jennings (6 July 1750 –26 Jan. 1760).

15. Letter 12, *An Authentic Narrative*, 80.

16. Newton to Jennings, 7 June 1754, MS #38.98(54) in Dr. Williams Library.

17. A web page (www.amazinggraceexperience.com) promoting a present tourist display in St.Kitts, honouring Newton's meetings with Clunie on the island, states that Clunie had brought a cargo that included 'gun powder for the major fortress Brimstone Hill.'

in all this time, met with one acquaintance who could assist me.'[18] For about a month while they were docked, the two spent many hours together, sometimes till midnight and later. Within a week, Newton happily reported back to Jennings. 'I find my affections more lively, my grace more active and my evidences of assurance more clear than I ever yet attained to in my life.'[19] During those weeks, 'brother Clunie' (as Newton referred to him)[20] encouraged Newton to be more public in his faith and in praying.[21] Of immense significance, Newton was delivered from his fear of relapsing into his former apostasy. 'Now I began to understand the security of the covenant of grace, and expect to be preserved, not by my own power and holiness, but by the mighty power and promise of God, through faith in an unchangeable Saviour.'[22] Clunie also explained what was happening in Christian current events. 'He likewise gave me a general view of the state of religion, with the errors and controversies of the times (things to which I had been entirely a stranger).'[23] Or as he described later in a letter to Clunie, it was an introduction to the knowledge 'of men and things.'[24] No doubt this included aspects of the Great Evangelical Awakening, the leading evangelists (George Whitefield and John Wesley), and the corresponding division of Methodism.

---

18. Letter 13, *An Authentic Narrative*, 87, 88.

19. Newton to Jennings, 7 June 1754.

20. Newton to Jennings, 7 June 1754.

21. Letter 13, *An Authentic Narrative*, 87, 88.

22. Letter 13, *An Authentic Narrative*, 87, 88.

23. Letter 13, *An Authentic Narrative*, 88.

24. Newton to Clunie, 4 Feb. 1761, Newton (Clunie), 6.

Prior to those long conversations with Clunie, Newton was surprisingly unaware of the theological and denominational issues and controversies of the day. He admitted years later that he had been a solitary Christian. As their visits came to an end, Clunie wisely encouraged Newton, during his breaks between sailings, to visit specific churches, chapels and clergy in London. Of course, this included visiting Samuel Brewer, his pastor of Stepney Independent (Congregational) Meeting in east London.

It is curious that Dr. Jennings' correspondence with Newton had not included news of the Evangelical Revival and its preachers. Eight years later when Jennings died 1762, Newton made a revealing comment in his diary that probably explains it. 'It is but very lately I have heard of the death of my friend Dr. J, my first and for a long while my only Christian correspondent after the Lord was pleased to open my eyes.... He always behaved with great kindness and I truly respected him, but he had an unhappy prejudice against some persons and things, which prevented me finding that freedom with him which I wished for.' Newton continued, 'In other respects he was a good man, and formerly very useful but, from the time he was displeased with the methods and instruments by which the Lord has been pleased to carry on his work of late years, his talents had less visible success than the much inferior qualifications of some whom he could not approve.' So because Jennings disagreed with what he saw in the Revival he remained aloof from it and hence did not discuss it with Newton. 'A stain of infirmity will appear in the best characters,' Newton acknowledged, 'and the Lord has been pleased to shew of late very remarkably that the success of his gospel does not depend at all upon the greatest attainments in human learning, but on administration of the Spirit and power from himself which he can give to whom he pleases and which he does give in a remarkable degree at present to many who have nothing else to depend on.'[25]

Newton sailed from St. Kitts on 20 June 1754 and in early August arrived safely back in Liverpool.[26] His employer, Joseph Manesty, who was just finishing the construction of a ship, now promised it to him. After the ship christening ceremony, at which Newton named it *Bee*, he set off for Chatham to spend his leave with Polly.[27] When they returned to Liverpool in October, he oversaw preparing of the *Bee* for her maiden voyage. But a few days before sailing, as Newton and Polly were casually sipping tea at home, he suffered something of an epileptic seizure and his physician advised him not to proceed. Manesty agreed and Newton resigned his command, just two days before the *Bee* was to sail.[28] Consequently in early November 1754, for twenty-nine-year-old Newton his life (eighteen years) on the seas was suddenly over. He would later learn that the captain who replaced him, most of the officers and many of the crew were killed in an uprising of slaves on-board the *Bee* as it was about to set sail.[29]

---

25. Diary [2] 6 Nov. 1762.

26. *Works*, 1:46.

27. Aitken, *Newton*, 124, 125.

28. Diary [1], page 158. Later, Newton found this blank page in his diary so he inserted a summary of what had happened. Here Newton says he resigned two days before the *Bee* was to sail, though in 1763, in his *An Authoritative Narrative*, he says it was the day before she was to set sail (Letter 13).

29. Letter 13, *An Authoritative Narrative*, 89; Aitken, *Newton*, 126.

Upon learning of this, he saw this as one more sign of God protecting him, but was not certain for what.

George Whitefield

George Whitefield was born in Gloucester, England, on 16 December 1714 at his parent's *The Bell Inn*. After his father died when George was two, his mother and older siblings managed the inn. He attended St. Mary de Crypt School attached to the church. It was there that he developed a love of drama; this would later influence his preaching style. In 1732 and just short of age eighteen, he entered Pembroke College, Oxford and supported himself by working as 'serviter' or student serving wealthier students. About a year later, he met John Wesley and his brother Charles (1707-1788) who were both part of the 'holy club' (as it was dubbed by others). This club of about ten graduate and undergraduate students was led by John Wesley. They followed a rigid regimen of study and lifestyle, and focused on spiritual exercises. Sadly, their intent was to earn favour of God. Charles invited George to the club and later loaned him a copy of *Life of God in the Soul of Man* by Henry Scougal. That book jolted him. 'God showed me that I must be born again or be damned.'[30] This radical concept launched him on an exhausting search to experience the new birth. Finally, after weeks of intense striving and exhaustion, he experienced release in early June 1735.[31] 'God was pleased to remove the heavy load, to enable me to lay hold of his dear Son by a living faith, and by giving me the Spirit of adoption, to seal me, even to

---

30. Dallimore, *Whitefield* (1990), 18.

31. Tyerman, *Whitefield*, 1: 32.

the day of everlasting redemption.'[32] This was three years before John and Charles experienced the same.[33]

On 14 October 1735, the two Wesley brothers sailed for the American colony of Georgia at Colonel Oglethorpe's invitation. Charles was to be the secretary to the Colonel (who was the founder of the Georgia colony and commander of the troops to protect the settlers) and John to be the chaplain to the settlers.[34] Hence Whitefield took over leadership of the club. In June 1736 (at the young age of twenty-one), he was ordained a deacon in the Established Church (also known as the Church of England or Anglican) and the following Sunday he preached at his home church, Church of St. Mary de Crypt, in Gloucester. The next month, he graduated and planned to take graduate studies at Oxford. But his plans were interrupted when John Wesley in Georgia, sent a general appeal to the Holy Club asking for more help to come. Charles was exhausted and on his way back to England. John sent a second letter to Whitefield and challenged him 'what if thou art the man, Mr. Whitefield.' Whitefield comments, 'upon reading it, my heart leaped within me, and, as it were, echoed the call.'[35] When the call became clearer, he resolved to go to Georgia as soon as possible. But problems in the arrangements delayed the voyage for almost a year. During this time of waiting, he returned to preach

---

32. Dallimore, *Whitefield* (1990),18.

33. Charles Wesley on 21 May 1738 and John Wesley on 24 May 1738.

34. Luke Tyerman, *The Life of the Rev. John Wesley* , 2 vols.(3rd. ed., London, 1876), 1:116; 'Timeline of John Wesley,' Museum of Methodism, Wesley Chapel, London, ‹ http://www.wesleyschapel.org.uk/timeline.htm› [accessed 20 Jan 2013].

35. Dallimore, *Whitefield*, 1: 107.

in Bristol where he had preached before with much success. His dynamic style was a welcomed contrast to the dull moralistic sermons of the time. Consequently crowds flocked to hear him, as they had earlier when he supplied for a couple of months in London. He wrote, 'Sometimes almost as many would go away for want of room as came in.'[36] After a month preaching there five times a week, he returned to London where he preached about nine times a week. Everywhere he preached, his sermons caused quite a stir (mostly positive but some negative). He wrote, possibly with youthful overstatement, that he was forced to travel by coach, rather than by foot, 'to avoid the hosannas of the multitude.'[37] He published nine of his sermons and sailed for Georgia in January 1738. This would be his first of seven mission trips to America. [38]

During his four month stay in Georgia, he became burdened to establish an orphanage for the orphans of settlers. This would become *Bethesda* (meaning House of Mercy) so he returned to England to make the arrangements and raise funds. For the rest of his life he would be a tireless fundraiser for his and others' causes. Once home he was ordained a priest[39] and set out for a preaching tour

---

36. Dallimore, *Whitefield*, 27.

37. Quoted in Boyd Stanley Schlenther, 'Whitefield, George (1714– 1770)', *Oxford Dictionary of National Biography*, Oxford University Press, 2004; online edn., May 2010 <http://www.oxforddnb.com/ view/article/29281>[accessed 13 Dec 2013].

38. 1) Jan. – Nov. 1738; 2) Aug. 1739 to March 1741; 3) Aug. 1744 to June, 1748; 4) Sept. 1751 – May 1752; 5) March, 1754 to May, 1755; 6) June 4, 1763 to July 8, 1765; 7) Sept., 1769 – Sept., 1770.

39. His being ordained a deacon, about two years earlier, was preliminary to becoming a priest.

through Wales. Stopping on the way in Bristol, where some clergy refused their pulpits, he preached to the miners in Kingswood, near Bristol. On Saturday 17 February 1739 Whitefield took the radical step to preach in the open air to coal miners who had no church nearby. Each day the crowds grew larger. This preaching in the open air 'was the turning point not only in his life but also in the history of evangelism,' and was two months before John Wesley reluctantly did the same.[40] Thereafter, Whitefield did not confine himself to the permission of local clergy, some of whom were opposed to his message and methods. Mark Noll makes this observation about Whitefield's preaching. 'Whitefield's great effect arose from what he proclaimed about the need for the new birth, but even more from how he proclaimed it – urgently, immediately and as the great question for every hearer *right now.*'[41]

He sailed on his second mission to America, August 1739; this time landing to the north in Delaware in October, almost a year since his first visit to the colonies. He started by preaching in and around Philadelphia and New York. By the end of this whirlwind visit he had preached in all the main colonies and in all the major cities. He triumphantly travelled up and down the coast, to immense crowds (over twenty thousand thronged to hear him in the Boston Common).[42] In his preaching

40. Michael Haykin, *The Revived Puritan: The Spirituality of George Whitefield* (Dundas, Ont., 2000), 29, 232n26.

41. Mark Noll, *The Rise of Evangelicalism: The Age of Edwards, Whitefield and the Wesleys* (Downers Grove, Ill., 2003), 88.

42. Noll, *The Rise of Evangelicalism*, 104.

journeys to the south he also launched the building of his orphanage (*Bethesda*) near Savannah. In the north, he preached for Jonathan Edwards in Northampton. 'His tours during this single visit from England remain among the most remarkable events in American religious history.'[43] This fifteen-month tour 'marked the beginning of the Great Awakening' in the colonies.[44] On the popular level, 'Whitefield had become the most famous person in America.'[45]

But when he arrived back in London in March 1741, he had to deal with his strained relationship with John and Charles Wesley. In April 1739, just prior to Whitefield's second mission to America, Wesley had preached a sermon in Bristol entitled *Free Grace*[46] in which he spoke against the Calvinist doctrines of 'unconditional election, irresistible grace and the final perseverance of the saints.'[47] These were doctrines that Whitefield had come to adopt, so before sailing he corresponded with John and Charles and sought to avoid a public split.[48] He acknowledged their differences as mentioned in the sermon, including John pressing for Christian

---

43. Noll, *The Rise of Evangelicalism*, 104.

44. Milton J. Coulter, 'Whitefield, George', DEB, 1180-1181.

45. Schlenther, 'Whitefield,'ODNB.

46. *Free Grace: A Sermon Preached in Bristol* (Bristol, 1739). For this conflict see, Kenneth J. Collins, 'Wesley's life and ministry,' in Randy L. Maddox and Jason E. Vickers, eds., *The Cambridge Companion to John Wesley* (Cambridge, 2010), 52, 53; Noll, *Rise of Evangelicalism*, 122, 123; Dallimore, *Whitefield*, 2:19 - 65.

47. Collins, 'Wesley's life and ministry,' 52.

48. Unless otherwise stated, in this paragraph I am following the sequence of correspondence and events in Kidd, *Whitefield*, 78-80, 144-147.

Perfection,[49] but urged John not to drag this into the public sphere where it would fuel rumours of animosity between them. But John had cast lots about this and felt convinced the results confirmed not only what he believed but also that he was to publish it. The sermon had been printed in Bristol though it is not certain when it was actually distributed in 1739.[50] Whenever it was in that year, Wesley reprinted this controversial sermon early in 1740 and again early 1741, while Whitefield was in America.[51] So Whitefield, now back in England, again sought reconciliation. But when it was obvious no agreement could be made, he published a letter he had written three months earlier, but not made public in England so as not to aggravate the situation.[52] It was titled '*A letter to the Rev. Mr. John Wesley in Answer to his Sermon "Free Grace"*.'[53] In the end, 'parties of both Calvinist and Wesleyan Methodists formed around the two leaders,' though by 1742 the relations between Whitefield and John Wesley were 'again cordial' though somewhat strained.[54]

Two others developments occurred while Whitefield had been away on his mission to America (August 1739-March 1741). Prior to this, in May 1738 the

---

49. Haykin, *The Revived Puritan*, 53-57.

50. For example, Collins, ('Wesley's life and ministry,' 52) says it was first published in April 1739 but Whitefield's letters in 1739 (25 June; 2 July) give the impression the sermon had not yet been printed, or at least not distributed (Kidd, *Whitefield*, 79, 80, 277n86).

51. Dallimore, *Whitefield*, 2:27n2.

52. Collins, 'Wesley's life and ministry,' 53.

53. It was published in London, 1741, with preface dated 9 August. The full letter is reprinted in Dallimore, *Whitefield*, 2:551-569.

54. Coulter, 'Whitefield, George', *DEB*, 1181.

Methodists and Moravians had formed a society in London for fellowship and prayer. But late in 1739, Wesley broke his connections with the Moravian-led Fetter Lane Religious Society. He and his colleagues purchased a former cannon factory (hence the term *The Foundery*) in Moorfields, London.[55] They renovated it to hold a congregation of 1,500, serve as headquarters and provide smaller rooms for class meetings. In early 1741, Whitefield's supporters built a large wooden structure that Whitefield called a Tabernacle to serve their London congregation. Tyerman points out that construction began before Whitefield had landed back in England from his second tour.[56] It too was in Moorfields where Whitefield had preached with great success.[57] But it was less than a quarter of a mile from the Foundery.[58] Edwin Welch states that Whitefield's supporters built it close to the Foundery because they 'undoubtedly wanted a meeting place as a counter-attraction to the Foundery.' However, he notes that 'Whitefield regretted that the Tabernacle was so close to the Foundery.'[59] Further, at the end of that year Whitefield hinted that it might be moved. 'We have a large society, consisting of several hundreds, a noble place to meet in; I have called it a *Tabernacle*, because,

---

55. Noll, *The Rise of Evangelicalism*, 120.

56. Tyerman, *Whitefield*, 1: 465, 484, 485.

57. Especially in July 1739. Tyerman, *Whitefield*, 1: 271.

58. Dallimore, *Whitefield*, 2:357. See map in J. Keith Cheetham, *On the Trail of John Wesley* (Glasgow, 2003), 8.

59. Welch, ed., *Two Calvinistic Methodist Chapels 1743-1811.* <(http://www.british-history.ac.uk/report.aspx?compid=38767>[accessed Jan. 11, 2014].

perhaps, we may be called to move our tents.'[60] But it was never moved.

Nevertheless, Whitefield was on the move. He responded to invitations from Scotland and went there from July to October 1741. This would be the first of his fifteen preaching missions to Scotland.[61] After one of these later missions to Scotland, he excitedly reported that 'In Scotland the word ran and was glorified; and in the North of England some fallow ground was ploughed up.' The results were encouraging but he longed for greater harvest. 'Oh to be made a New threshing Instrument having teeth! I am an ambitious Creature. Feign w^d I thresh the Mountains.'[62] Just prior to his first mission to Scotland, he had met Mrs. Elizabeth James, a widow in Wales who was a close friend of the Welsh evangelist, Howell Harris.[63] Harris had recommended they meet, in the hopes that Whitefield would marry her. During the tour in Scotland, Whitefield corresponded with her, and upon his return they were married 14 November 1741.

---

60. See letter, 7 Dec. 1741, Gillies, *Whitefield Works*, 1:344.

61. Dallimore, *Whitefield* (1990), 66 says fifteen, though Schlenther, 'Whitefield,'*ODNB* says fourteen.

62. Whitefield to Mrs. Leighton, (14 Oct. 1762), Mrs. Leighton's Letter Book (Box CO 5, Folder 7), David M. Rubenstein Library Rare Book & Manuscript Library, Duke University. For more details on Mrs. Leighton and Whitefield's letters to her, see upcoming article, Grant Gordon, 'A Revealing Unpublished Letter of George Whitefield to John Collett Ryland,' *Baptist Quarterly*, April 2016 [proposed title and date].

63. Actually she was more than a friend. Harris loved her but believed that marriage would hinder his closeness to God (Dallimore, *Whitefield* [1990], 112-115). See also Kidd, *Whitefield*, 157-159.

Seven months later he returned to Scotland after hearing of a revival breaking out in Cambuslang where he had preached. He arrived in June 1742 near the peak of the revival and began preaching immediately. The services attracted thousands, ever increasing, and in one meeting in the fields, he preached to twenty thousand and the service lasted well into the night. Whitefield concluded, 'it far out-did all I ever saw in America.'[64] The next day, he preached on 'Thy Maker Is Thy Husband,' which historian Stout declares, 'by many accounts, this was the most powerful sermon of the revival.'[65]

He returned south to continue extensive itinerating and strengthening the organisation of the Calvinistic Methodists. But it was time to return to America, as he had been away for four years, so he and Elizabeth sailed for America, landing 26 October 1744 in York, New Hampshire. On arrival he had to address fanaticism that had broken out, for which he was blamed. Despite this and increasing opposition the Awakening continued. Travelling south along the coast he preached to large crowds in many places, including Boston, New York city, and Philadelphia. Reaching Georgia he was delighted to see the progress of construction of his Orphan House and the development of the grounds. On this mission trip he preached extensively in the Southern and Middle Colonies. But all this continuous travelling took its toll on his health. So when time came for him to return to England, he chose to first go to Bermuda

---

64. Harry S. Stout, *The Divine Dramatist: George Whitefield and the Rise of Modern Evangelicalism* (Grand Rapids, Mich., 1991), 149.

65. Stout, *The Divine Dramatist*, 149.

for about a month to do some preaching and to recover from exhaustion.[66]

Over the next eight years (1748-1755) he made two more trips to America (his fourth and fifth). In these he maintained a gruelling travelling preaching schedule, as well as devoting time for his beloved *Bethesda*. On his fifth visit, the positive response he received during his tour of New England brought back fond memories of the first time he had ministered there. At Old North meeting house in Boston, the church was so packed he had to enter through a window. In appreciation of his many efforts on the school's behalf, Princeton[67] awarded him an honorary M.A. degree. Whitefield wrote back to Gillies in Scotland, 'my reception has been far superior to that of fourteen years ago.'[68] On 27 March he sailed from America and landed 8 May 1755 at Newhaven on the south-east coast of England. He would not return to America for eight years, in part, because the Seven Years War (1756-1763) made travel dangerous. He was now about to enter his longest period of ministry in his homeland.

---

66. He left Elizabeth in America to oversee Bethesda, but she returned to England months later (Kidd, *Whitefield*, 201-203).

67. At that time it was called College of New Jersey.

68. This quote and details in the paragraph are from Stout, *The Divine Dramatist*, 218.

2

London Area (1754-1755)

Resting In Chatham and Visits to London

After quitting the sea, John and Mary (Polly) returned to
Chatham in Kent, thirty-five miles south-east of London
where he could recuperate and they would be with her
family and friends in her hometown. While there during
the next nine months, Newton took frequent opportunity
to visit London so he could hear many of the preachers
that Clunie had mentioned. Finally he could now have the
kind of Christian fellowship he had missed while on the
high seas. Most of the preachers and mid-week lecturers
he heard were Dissenters, especially Independents/Con-
gregationalists and Presbyterians.[1] He periodically heard
Dr. Jennings who was pastor of the Independent Meeting
at Old Gravel Lane. As mentioned earlier, Jennings had
been the pastor of Newton's mother. He had also been
a close friend of the great hymn-writer Isaac Watts. Another was Samuel Hayward,[2] the Congregational pastor at
Silver Street who, every other midweek, gave lectures at
the Presbyterian meeting at Little St. Helen's, Bishopsgate.

---

1. See Hindmarsh, *Newton*, 69, 70 for a list of places and preachers.

2. Samuel Hayward (1718-1757) and Samuel Pike (1717-1773) pub-
    lished their lectures in 1755 as *Some Important Cases of Conscience
    Answered, at the Casuistical Exercise, on Wednesday Evenings, in Little St.
    Helen's, Bishopsgate-Street.*

He frequently heard Samuel Brewer[3] (1723-1796) who served as pastor of the Stepney Independent Meeting House[4] just a mile from Jennings. Brewer would eventually serve Stepney for fifty years. Captain Clunie was a member of this congregation that was, according to William Phipps, the largest Congregational church in London.[5] Brewer, who was only two years older than Newton, became his close friend and primary early mentor. So much so that a decade later, in *An Authentic Narrative*, he said of Brewer, 'From him I received many helps both in public and private; for he was pleased to favour me with his friendship from the first. His kindness and the intimacy between us have continued to this day; and of all my many friends, I am most deeply indebted to him.'[6] Both Brewer and Hayward were supporters of the Revival. For Brewer this began in his mid-teens when he enthusiastically attended the London outdoor preaching of Whitefield. His biographer mentions that on one occasion, Brewer's tutor was so upset with Brewer and a classmate attending Whitefield's preaching that when they returned, he 'inflicted a disgraceful punishment' on them and sent them to their rooms without

---

3. See 'Life of Rev. Samuel Brewer,' *Evangelical Magazine* (1797): 5-18.

4. The Stepney Meeting-House was almost opposite St. Dunstans. The present church called Stepney Meeting, which is now amalgamated with John Knox Chapel, is lower down Stepney Way near Jubilee Street (Cecil/Rouse, *Newton*, 89, 90).

5. Phipps, *Amazing Grace in John Newton*, 67.

6. Letter 14, *An Authentic Narrative*, 90.

any food.[7] Yet rather than deter Brewer it reinforced his awareness of the deadness of the 'frigid orthodoxy' of his tutor and the inspiring eloquence of Whitefield.

Newton also heard various preachers at Whitefield's Tabernacle[8] in Moorfields. Two years before Newton's visit, this large brick building in East London had been built to replace the earlier wooden Tabernacle. Although that first wooden structure built in 1741 had shielded Whitefield's hearers from the wind and rain, Tyerman described it as 'at best, it was a huge ugly shed'.[9] In contrast, this new brick building was eighty by eighty with surrounding galleries and could hold 4,000 worshippers. There they gathered to hear Whitefield when he was not on one of his many itinerant preaching tours.[10]

---

7. 'Life of Rev. Samuel Brewer,' *Evangelical Magazine* (1797): 6, 7.

8. Built in 1753 this building would serve until 1786 when it was replaced by a smaller stone structure at the corner of Leonard and Tabernacle streets. However, services were discontinued here in the early 1930s when the area became more commercial. The building still stands (Dallimore observed in 1990 that it was used as a gymnasium for a nearby school) and the memorial stone on the outside says, 'Near this spot stood the Tabernacle built by Rev. George Whitefield in 1753.' See Dallimore, *Whitefield* 1:355-357, 2:546; Dallimore, *Whitefield* (1990), 183, 184. For pictures of the Tabernacle see Johnston, *Whitefield*, 2:482, 483; Dallimore, *Whitefield*, following page 2:144. See Welch, *Two Calvinistic Methodist Chapels*. <http://www.british-history.ac.uk/report.aspx?compid=38767> [accessed Jan. 11, 2014]. Welch, n.36 states that the first Tabernacle lay to the west of Windmill Hill (now Tabernacle Street). For picture see p. 120.

9. Tyerman, *Whitefield*, 2:290.

10. Dallimore, *Whitefield*, 2:357; *Whitefield* (1990), 184.

In contrast, it would not be until 1778 that Wesley built a more lasting meeting house and headquarters, to replace his original Foundery.[11]

Despite the doctrinal differences between Whitefield and the Wesleys, there was now renewed co-operation between them.[12] During construction of the new Tabernacle, Whitefield's congregation continued to meet in the old Tabernacle while the new one was being built around it.[13] But it appears that at least on one occasion Whitefield's congregation had the use of one of Wesley's chapels.[14] To Charles he writes, 'My Dear friend, I thank you and your brother most heartily for the loan of the chapel,'[15] and in

---

11. Today the Wesley Chapel, at 49 City Road, is a very attractive and well-cared-for building with an active congregation. Over the years, stained-glass windows have been installed and the pillars (that were ship masts donated by King George III) supporting the gallery have been replaced by jasper pillars donated from Methodist bodies overseas. Many consider it the Cathedral of Methodism. In the crypt beneath is now a Museum of Methodism and next door is the home where Wesley lived. Both are open for tours. Behind is John Wesley's tomb and opposite lies the Bunhill Fields Burial Grounds where Susanna Wesley (John's mother) is buried. Many notable Nonconformists are buried there, including John Bunyan, George Fox, John Gill, John Owen, John Rippon and Isaac Watts.

12. Johnston, *Whitefield*, 2:260, especially Whitefield's letter, 10 March 1753.

13. Tyerman, *Whitefield*, 2:291, quoting Seymour, *Life and Times of Selina, Countess of Huntingdon* (London, 1844), 1:203.

14. It is not clear to which chapel Whitefield is referring. Dallimore, *Whitefield*, 2:356n suggests it was Wesley's West Street Chapel. The West Street Chapel (established in 1743), a former Huguenot chapel, was Wesley's first chapel in London's West End. The site is near the present Cambridge Circus, but it is no longer used as a church (*Methodist Heritage Handbook 2010*, Methodist Church House, p. 18). However, Robert Philip in Philip, *Whitefield*, 409 says it was Spitalfields Chapel. Neither Dallimore nor Philip substantiates their comment.

15. Whitefield to Charles Wesley, March 3, 1753 cited in Tyerman, *Whitefield*, 2:298.

the letter he includes not only how the construction was progressing but also provides family news. Adjoining the Tabernacle was the Tabernacle House for Whitefield and his wife Elizabeth.[16] In conjunction with the opening of the new Tabernacle, Whitefield compiled and published a hymnbook *Hymns for Social Worship ... for Use of the Congregation in London* (1753) containing one hundred and seventy hymns, plus some composed doxologies. Many were written by Isaac Watts, but there were also at least twenty-five by the Wesleys. It was well received and went through thirty-six editions.[17] Another sign of their friendship is that in December of that year, Whitefield cut short his preaching tour when he heard that John Wesley was dying. To the Selina Hastings, Countess of Huntingdon (1707-1791), he wrote, 'I am now hastening to London, to pay my last respects to my dying friend.'[18] Ironically, Wesley recovered and lived another forty years, far outliving Whitefield.

This Tabernacle is not to be confused with Whitefield's larger Tottenham Court Road chapel[19] built near the theatre district in London the year after Newton's first visit. Edwin Welch states that 'Whitefield regretted

---

16. Dallimore, *Whitefield*, 2:357, 386.

17. Tyerman, *Whitefield*, 2:294, 295. Tyerman points out that soon after in that year, Wesley also published a hymnbook for his own congregation. See also Dallimore, *Whitefield* (1990), 357.

18. Quoted in Johnston, *Whitefield*, 2:274 (3 Dec. 1753).

19. Tottenham Court Road chapel was built in 1756 at the corner of Tottenham Court Road and Googe Street. Unfortunately, near the end of WW2 it was destroyed by a German V2 rocket. A smaller structure (with the name Whitefield Memorial Church engraved above the entrance door) was built on the site. Now it is the location of the American International Church (new name as of 2013) which is a congregation of the United Reformed Church that owns the building (79a Tottenham Court Road). See Dallimore, *Whitefield*, 2: 383-399,546, 547; Johnston, *Whitefield*, 2:575, 576; For pictures, see Dallimore, *Whitefield*, 2:305 (in 1772) and Johnston, *Whitefield* , 2:483, 484 (as it stands today).

that the Moorfields Tabernacle was so close to the Foundery and built the Tottenham Court Road chapel in 1756 for this reason.'[20] Beneath that Chapel, Whitefield had a vault built where he desired that he and both Wesleys would be interred. He boldly declared this plan to the bigoted members of his congregation. 'We will all lie together. You will not let them enter your chapel while they are alive. They can do no harm when they are dead.'[21] However, as it later turned out, this wish could not be fulfilled, though his wife Elizabeth was buried there in 1768. When the Tottenham Chapel was completed and Whitefield was not on his tours, he preached at both Chapel and Tabernacle each Sunday. Large numbers, many from elite and influential families, attended the Chapel and within three years, it had to be enlarged. The expanded structure was one hundred and twenty-seven feet long, seventy feet wide and with a dome a hundred and fourteen feet high.Dallimore comments it was 'undoubtedly the largest Dissenting church anywhere in the world and was known as "The Dissenters' Cathedral." '[22]

Newton also heard evangelical preachers in the Established Church. One was William Romaine (1714-1795) who at the time was a lecturer at St. Dunstan's and assistant morning preacher at St. George's, Hanover Square in the fashionable district of London. Later in 1766, he became the rector of St. Anne's, Blackfriars where he

---

20. Welch, *Two Calvinistic Methodist Chapels* <http://www.british-history.ac.uk/report.aspx?compid=38767> [accessed Jan. 11, 2014].

21. Tyerman, *Whitefield*, 2:373.

22. Dallimore, *Whitefield*, 2:547.

had a very influential ministry for thirty years.[23] Newton maintained his connection with the Established Church by once a month receiving the sacrament. When Hayward informed Newton of the extraordinary spiritual work in the Established Church at Cornwall especially through the ministry of Samuel Walker (1714-1761)[24] of Truro, and showed Newton two of Walker's letters, he was moved to write in his diary: 'Saw two of his letters, wrote* in a charming spirit indeed; so much zeal, and so much charity and humility, as can never reside in the same heart unless they are inspired from above.' In response he concluded, 'It is my duty to pray that the Lord may own him more and more; and especially as a member of the Established Church I ought to pray that the number of such faithful labourers* may be increased and that it would please God to revive that spirit which has been so long greatly departed from us.'[25] Little did he know that nine

---

23. Later when Newton moved to St. Mary Woolnoth, London, in 1780, he noted that Romaine was the only other evangelical clergy who had an Established Church of his own in the city. At the time, the other evangelical Established clergy in London were assistants, chaplains or lecturers. Later, Newton spoke highly of Romaine's character and ministry. 'Mr. Romaine was fifty-eight years in the ministry, an honourable and useful man, inflexible as an iron pillar in publishing the truth, and unmoved either by the smiles or the frowns of the world. He was the most popular man of the Evangelical party since Mr. Whitefield, and few remaining will be more missed' (Bull, *Newton*, 245, 246, 328). For a recent biography, see Tim Shenton, *An Iron Pillar: The Life and Times of William Romaine* (Darlington, 2004).

24. For a recent biography, see Tim Shenton, *A Cornish Revival: The Life and Times of Samuel Walker of Truro* (Darlington, 2002).

25. Diary [1], 28 March 1755.

years later, he himself would become one of those labourers in the Established Church.

When back home in Chatham he continued his spiritual reading. In January 1755, Newton read a 'journal and
a defence' by John Wesley. These could have been the ex-
tracts of Wesley's journal Nov 1746 to July 1750 (1754) and
Free Grace that had a 4th edition published in 1754. Though
Hindmarsh says 'there were several tracts related to the
Calvinistic controversy published 1754/55 which could be
the 'defence' referred to by Newton.[26] To these Newton reflected, 'know not what to say of his account of the manner
in which so many of his hearers were awakened; only that
I never met with any instance of the kind I could depend
on.' Despite his caution, he admitted the good. 'Yet there
seems to be a spirit of sincerity and gospel zeal for gospel
truths in his writing; and be the errors of him or his followers what they will, I believe God has been pleased to make
him an instrument of good. Lord carry on and increase thy
work in thy own way and teach me to honour a principle
of grace wherever I find it, though mixed as it must more or
less [be] with human weakness.'[27]

Four days later, Newton read some letters of Whitefield and commented: 'Some letters I have met with of
Mr. Whitefield and others have led me to adore the free
grace of God in them and while my heart was warm I submitted myself to the guidance of the same spirit.' Yet he
cautioned himself. 'Though I have no cause to subscribe
myself [one of] their followers, yet I cannot but admire
and respect many of them for I know not where I found

26. Hindmarsh, *Newton*, 334.

27. Diary [1], 21 Jan 1755..

such expressions of love to God and man; such marks of humility and zeal for the glory of the gospel, as amongst them.'[28] In May he loaned a friend his book of Whitefield's sermons.[29] Yet soon he would hear Whitefield for himself.

Whitefield Preaches In London

When Newton learned that Whitefield had returned to London from his fifth mission to America,[30] he jumped at the opportunity to rush back to London so that he might hear, and hopefully meet, the famed preacher at his Moorfields Tabernacle. Newton outlined his plan in his diary:

> 'Thursday 5 June. I proposed on Sunday to go to London this day to visit my Christian friends there and to particularly with a view of hearing at least, or if I can [of] getting the acquaintance of Mr. Whitefield. I pray that the Lord will direct my steps and direct my conversation to my good and his glory, and restore me home in peace and preserve all my concerns in my absence. Amen.'

This trip to London turned out to be most significant for Newton. So on his return home a week later, he carefully transposed his notes into his permanent diary. He began by exclaiming that 'mercy and goodness followed me all the way' and then recorded what he had heard.[31]

Editor's Note: Unless indicated otherwise, what follows is Newton's complete diary notes covering this visit

---

28. Diary [1], 25 January 1755. Possibly this was Whitefield's '*A letter to the Rev. Mr. John Wesley in Answer to his Sermon "Free Grace".*'

29. Diary [1], 20 May 1755.

30. Whitefield landed at Newhaven on the southern shore and directly south of London, 8 May 1755 (Tyerman, 2:340).

31. The following was written on Friday, June 13, the day after his return home from London.

to London, 6 June – 12 June 1755. He filled up each page and gave very few breaks. Therefore, to assist present readers follow more easily, the sermons have been numbered, the King James text added, sermon points have been separated and long sections are divided into paragraphs. Where not obvious, Newton's personal reflections have been italicised by the editor to distinguish them from Whitefield's sermon. A single asterisk indicates Newton's spelling. Material or comments in square brackets have been added by the editor.

'Fryday* [6 June, 1755] having greatly fatigued laid in till near 8. After breakfast went to Mr. Brewer's; spent an hour with him and by his advice and in his name waited upon Mr. Whitefield. But he being engaged in pressing business,[32] I was obliged to take my leave so soon. The afternoon at Mr. Hayward's. He gave me a letter to Mr. Whitefield, as a testimonial for the sacrament.[33] Heard him [Whitefield] preach in the evening on the new birth, from **Rev. 21:5**.

[SERMON 1]

[⁵And he that sat upon the throne said, Behold, I make all things new. And he said unto me, Write: for these words are true and faithful.]

I shall not here insert the heads of his discourses, which is no suitable way of judging Mr. Whitefield's preaching,

---

32. Newton, in what appears to be a letter to his wife Polly, writes: 'Introduc'd myself to Mr. Whitefield at his own house, he receiv'd me very kindly, but was just finishing some letters to go to Carolina by a vessel that sails this afternoon so I was forc'd to decamp from thence' (Martin, *Newton*, 147, but not footnoted).

33. Visitors were required to get an approved ticket of admission to the sacrament (Philip, *Whitefield*, 297). See Newton's comment, 8 June 1755.

though I propose to commit to writing the most striking of his thoughts in the different times I heard him. However, this I say, that he described the reality and necessity of a change of heart in a very powerful manner indeed. After [the] sermon [I] delivered the letter; but he was so engaged in company he could neither read that nor several others given to him, but desired I would call in the morning.

Saturday. [7 June] Rose early; found my frame growing warmer. Went to get the answer to the letter, and received in consequence a ticket for admission to the communion. I had about five minutes converse with Mr. Whitefield then, and he excused himself in a very friendly, obliging manner from anything farther, upon account of his throng of business.

Spent the day at Mr. C.[34] and in the evening returned to the Tabernacle;[35] heard the preparation sermon, from **Lev. 10:3**.

[SERMON 2]

[**[3]Then Moses said unto Aaron, This is it that the LORD spake, saying, I will be sanctified in them that come nigh me, and before all the people I will be glorified. And Aaron held his peace.**]

How aw[e]ful[36] and how comfortable a discourse, when he spoke of the different ways of coming near to God,

---

34. Probably either John (Jack) Catlett (1731-1764), his brother-in-law who became a solicitor in London (Cecil/Rouse, *Newton*, 274; Martin, *Newton*, 203) or Captain Clunie.

35 Orig. 'the T_'.

36. Newton spells it *awful*, which in the eighteenth century meant inspiring reverential fear and wonder; aweful.

and what was meant by sanctifying Him, with the danger of neglecting it.

I hope it was laid to my heart. I went home and prayed with more than usual fervency for a blessing on the ordinance in which I had undertaken to draw near to God, etc.; then went to bed without engaging in any conversation that might interrupt my views.

[SERMON 3]

Sunday. [8 June] Rose at 4. After private prayer, etc., went to the Tabernacle; was admitted upon producing the ticket and here indeed I had a blessing. There were about a 1,000 or more people of different persuasions, but all agreed in the great essentials of the gospel, and in mutual charity worshipping the Lord with one heart and soul. Never before had I such an idea and foretaste of the business of heaven. Mr. Whitefield made use of the office [i.e. liturgy] of the Church of England,[37] interspersing exhortations, encouragement, etc., occasionally all along. And it seemed as though that composure, that elevation, and assurance of faith which shone in his frame and discourses was in some measure diffused over the whole assembly. He made many little intervals for singing. I believe near 20 times in all. I hope I shall have lasting reason to bless God for favouring me with such an opportunity. We were about three hours in the ordinance.

---

37. Following the Anglican order of the communion service was important to Whitefield. That year, he edited a 140-page book (*A Communion Morning's Companion*) that included meditations, the order for the administration of the Lord's Supper and fifty-nine sacramental hymns'(Tyerman, *Whitefield*, 2:344, 345).

At the end, I went away rejoicing from thence to Mr. Brewer's. Heard a stranger (to me) from Titus 1:1 on the marks of a true faith or the faith of God's elect, to all which I trust my conscience gave me humble answer of peace. In the afternoon Mr. Brewer [spoke on] Col 1:8 on the use and necessity of having wisdom and spiritual understanding to direct our zeal and love and prevent us from falling into error; a useful subject in these evil times.

From thence went to Mr. Whitefield again. A prodigious multitude of people, so that, besides those who staid*[38] in the yard, many hundreds were forced to go away, though the place is supposed to contain 5,000. His discourse was suited to the audience—an offer and pressing invitation to the gospel, from **Rev. 21:6**.

[SERMON 4]

[[6]And he said unto me, It is done. I am Alpha and Omega, the beginning and the end. I will give unto him that is athirst of the fountain of the water of life freely.]

And with great life and power he was carried out[39], though some are offended with his observing too little method in his discourses at these times, which I am well assured he does on purpose, and that this incoherent way (as it is called) of preaching has been owned in calling many souls to the gospel. For, in speaking more particularly to the cases and experience of believers he is methodical enough.

---

38. Bull changes this to 'stand' (Bull, *Newton*, 71).

39. The phrase 'carried out' was 'a common testimony of evangelical converts' in the revival; the feeling of having one's soul or spirit seemingly leaving the body to commune with God and savor his grace and love' (Kidd, *Whitefield*, 16).

After this general sermon he prayed, and discoursed again to the society.[40] And here he was most excellent in giving them charges with respect to moral and relative duties. I think, had any of his enemies been present, they must have acquitted him of many calumnies they have (some of them, I hope) been deceived into.

[Editor's note: Cornelius Winter who attended the Tabernacle and assisted him near the end of Whitefield's ministry describes these post-sermon sessions. 'The society, which after [the] sermon was encircled in the area of the Tabernacle, consisted of widows, married people, young men and spinsters, placed separately; all of whom when a considerable part of the congregation was re-settled, for hundreds to stay upon the occasion, used to receive from him in the colloquial style various exhortations comprised of short sentences, and suitable to their various stations.'][41]

In walking home was engaged with somebody concerning the extent of Christian charity (a subject I often find reason to stand up for). Though this day was hot and I was up early and walked a good deal, I was in better spirits and less tired or disposed to business[42] than usual. The frame of my mind, which was beyond what I ever perhaps knew before, enlivened my body and I went to bed in peace. Blessed be God for his goodness.

---

40. Beside the Tabernacle, there was a Society Room and attendance at this was restricted. See Dallimore, *Whitefield* (1990) 125-130 for description of how this was organised.

41. See 'Whitefield as seen through the eyes of a young assistant,' Dallimore, *Whitefield*, 2:486.

42. First part of word is unclear.

Monday [9 June] morning awoke and rose early, in a warm frame; begun the day in some measure suitable to what I experienced the day before. Breakfasted with Mr. Woolmer and went to Stratford with him to dinner.[43] We had much spiritual conversation and I hope I was enabled to offer something useful in my turn; at least careful to express a sense of God's undeserving goodness to me. And I endeavoured in particular that we might fortify each other against the fear of singularity,[44] so much as will [happen] in these days, fall to the lot of all who are desirous to walk according to the Gospel. Returned with him in the afternoon to Stepney where Mr. Brewer preached to the two religious societies an occasional[45] sermon from Heb. 10:23, 24; afterwards sup'd [with] them and had a very agreeable evening considering how many people there were.

Tuesday [10 June] morning rose at 4; had an hour in private with some comfort; called on Mr. Woolmer and went with him to hear Mr. Whitefield. He preached from **Psalm 142:7**, first part.

[SERMON 5]

[⁷**Bring my soul out of prison, that I may praise thy name: the righteous shall compass me about; for thou shalt deal bountifully with me.**]

---

43. Woolmer appears to have lived in Stratford (London), as mentioned in Newton's undated letter to Polly, quoted in full later. This Stratford is about 5 miles east of Moorfields and in the northeast section of the present Greater London and not to be confused with the more famous Stratford-upon-Avon.

44. Different from others; perceived eccentric.

45. An occasional sermon is one that is suited for a specific occasion or event.

It is hard or impossible for me to give a specimen of his discourse. His subject was concerning the various prisons a believer is liable to in his passing through life. He is naturally in prison in sin and in the body, and these bring him into various other straits, such as afflictions, temptations, desertions, and the grave; all which, from the confinement they lay us under, may be termed prisons. He afterwards spoke of the duty incumbent upon us when it pleases God to deliver us out of our temporary prisons and for His promise of freeing us from the power of the grave; We are to praise His name.

Something like this was his plan. But the power, the experience, the warmth with which he treated it I can by no means express, though I hope I feel something of it still; my heart was greatly impressed, and I had little relish either for company or victuals[46] all day.

After breakfast, was at Pinner's Hall.[47] Heard Mr. Rollins[48] from 2 Sam. 23:5 presenting a set of sermons he began when I was last in town. He confined himself in this [sermon] to speak of the everlasting nature of God's love to his people and here I perceived an inconvenience which would perhaps ensue was* I constantly to hear Mr. Whitefield preach, for though Mr.

---

46. Bull, *Newton*, 72, updated this to 'food' in his transcription of this sentence.

47. Pinner's Hall, in Old Broad Street since 1672, held a weekday lecture conducted by leading dissenting ministers in and about London (Bull, *Newton*, 68n).

48. Bull, *Newton*, transcribed this as Rawlins. This was actually Richard Rawlin (d. 1757) the Presbyterian pastor of Fetter-Lane, London and one of the appointed lecturers at Pinner's Hall. He is known for his 1741 publication of his lectures on justification, *Christ the Righteousness of his People: or, The Doctrine of Justification by Faith in Him*. For biographical sketch see the reprint (Glasgow, 1753), 5, 6.

R's discourse was very excellent, both for sound doctrine and comfortable application and I approved and admired it all. Yet my heart was absent, [because] the want of that lively address to the affections which I had found 2 or 3 hours before made me hear with some impatience. I had forgot* the blessing is only from God and [I] seemed inclined to place a personal dependence on Mr. Whitefield's ministry as though the Lord spoke by him only. And as I find something of this a complaint with others, methinks I see a beauty in dispensations of providence, which have adapted his gifts so suitably to his calling; for was* he constantly resident in one place, those who sat under him would run great risque* of resting in the ordinances[49] and despising the different gifts of others. Though on the other hand it is a great blessing that God has raised up a man so adapted to water,[50] to revive, to stir up and call in, and then sends from place to place for the general good. Retired this evening and went to bed betimes,[51] being as I said, greatly indisposed for company, but joy and peace within my own breast.

[Newton's many comments (e.g. [the] assurance of faith which shone in his frame and discourses ... the power, the experience, the warmth') clearly show that he had been overwhelmed by Whitefield's preaching and being in the services. As he says, it was 'a foretaste of the business of heaven.' Therefore, he wanted to stay in London longer than planned and informed Polly. He had much to share with her when he returned but he could not wait to

---

49. One meaning at the time was the *ordinance of preaching*.

50. No doubt a reference to Whitefield's many sailing journeys.

51. Early; in good time.

mention some of what he had experienced. One can sense his excitement as he writes to her.

'Do my dearest Polly excuse my staying till Thursday; some new engagements have offered for tomorrow, but I chiefly wait to hear Mr. Whitefield once more, which it is said will be the last time of his preaching till he returns from his circuit.[52] However, you may be assured that if he does [preach] oftener, neither he nor anybody else shall detain me from you another day. Hitherto I have been willing to strike while the iron is hot as the saying is, and indeed as I came up with a good design, so it has pleased God to bless it greatly to me. And without his blessing it signifies little who we hear.

But I am persuaded now I have tried, that there is something extraordinary in this persecuted despised man, beyond any common attainments, beyond any other person perhaps which the present or the former age has known.

I received the sacrament from him at the Tabernacle Sunday morning. There were none present but communicants and none of those, but such as having either passed a suitable examination of strangers or bringing sufficient vouchers from a minister whom he knew and could depend on, received a ticket of admission the day before. Yet notwithstanding this caution, I believe we were not less than twelve hundred people met together with one heart and soul, though of different forms and persuasions [being] church folks,[53] Baptists, Presbyterians, etc. In short, any that agreed in the grand fundamentals of our faith and [who] bore testimony of a suitable practice.

---

52. Soon after Whitefield set out on a three-week tour of west England (Tyerman, *Whitefield*, 2:345).

53. The Established Church/ Church of England.

He used the office of the Church of England, interspersing at times exhortations and discourses after the manner of the dissenters, and every ten minutes or oftener we stopped and sung part of a hymn, I suppose 20 different times in all or more. The number of persons, the beauty of singing, the decency and regularity of the whole service joined to the noble and enlivening views he led us into by his powerful and evangelical discourses, all these being blessed by God to my benefit, was such a resemblance and foretaste of heaven as it not possible to describe. I believe there were very few there who could not say, as the disciples of our Lord, 'did not our heart burn within us, while he talked to us'.[54] The service lasted 3 hours, though there was no sermon.

I have heard him preach 5 times, always in a different manner, according as he had a different view or a different audience. The last was this morning, which exceeded all the rest and it was really beyond my imagination. I believe there were hardly 10 people in the congregation, which was pretty large, of any seriousness at all, who could not refrain from tears; mine I am sure were the tears of joy. Mr. Brewer's eyes were full often and he was forced to hide his face. He and Mr. Hayward and many of the most owned and honoured preachers about town seize every opportunity of hearing him, though they come 2 or 3 miles, and they all say, they think themselves in a manner unfit and ashamed to go into a pulpit after [hearing] him.

I trust I shall, as you say in yours, be able to bring down something with me that may be useful to us both, and that I may be like the scribe well instructed who brings

---

54. Luke 24: 32.

out of his treasure things new and old.[55] I am sure I have enjoyed the rich opportunities for this purpose, for besides Mr. Whitefield, I have heard Mr. Brewer twice, Mr. Rollins and another once each. I spent the greatest part of yesterday with Mr. Woolmer at Stratford.

Thus, I have given you a little specimen beforehand. [I] shall add no more but my prayers and praises on your behalf; and respects to all with you.

I am my dearest Dear, your most affectionate and obliged.[56]

J. Newton.'][57]

Wednesday [11 June] rose early, breakfasted with Mr. Woolmer and spent the forenoon in spiritual discourse. Went to J.C.[58]; had near 2 hours argument with him, but forced to give it up as before. Though I think I was more enlarged and ready than usual, but the work is God's only. Lord, do thou be pleased to take it in hand for good. In the afternoon visited Mr. Pike,[59] had much

---

55. Matthew 13:52.

56. This is typical of Newton's periodic expressive phrases to Polly.

57. Transcription of most of this letter in Cecil/Rouse, *Newton*, 90, 91. I have included other details from the original manuscript letter (no date), MS 2935 (f. 218) at Lambeth Palace.

58. Probably John Catlett, his brother-in-law who was a solicitor in London. Newton often debated theological matters with him because he was wary of Methodists and evangelicalism (Cecil/Rouse, *Newton*, 273). See five of Newton's letters to him in Josiah Bull, ed. *Letters of John Newton with biographical sketches* (1869, Edinburgh reprint 2007), 22-37.

59. Probably Samuel Pike who alternated with Samuel Hayward giving the weekly lecture at Little St. Helen's, Bishopsgate.

pleasure in some experimental[60] conversation that was carried on there. Had an opportunity of declaring once more what God had done for my soul and received from him an account no less extraordinary than my own, of a person who had professed Deism and Freethinking with greater opportunities than I did and had accordingly appeared on that side [of] the question in print and had ever dared to write against the being of a God and many other things most grossly scandalous and profane. Yet now through rich sovereign grace depends entirely upon the Lord Jesus Christ whom he once persecuted. If I have opportunity, I think to get [more] acquainted with this fellow monument of free mercy.

From thence went to the Tabernacle for the last opportunity and heard a no less striking discourse than the former from **Numbers 12:9**.

[SERMON 6]

[⁹And the anger of the LORD was kindled against them; and he departed.]

After a pretty long paraphrase and observation upon the context, as is his way sometimes, he came to speak to the case of God's withdrawing his gracious presence from a believer and departing from him for a season; for a total and final departure (and blessed be God he said as it is written) we are freed from, by the covenant of grace and the assurance of his everlasting love. He shewed*:

1st the usual causes as spiritual pride, careless sinful walk, love of the world, vain conversation, waste of time and talents, etc.

---

60. Practical application to what they were discussing.

2nd the marks of it [being] barrenness and deadness with regard to duties and ordinances and remiss conduct, making light of small sins (as they are by some called), and at length a callous insensible disposition, which makes us think all [is] peace and well, while we are upon the brink of ruin. This in kind bordered upon total apostasy and would infallibly end in it could we be left to ourselves; but in such a state God will in mercy find us out and either by outward providences or spiritual humblings, bring[61] us to seek him again and feel and acknowledge it to be an evil and a bitter thing that ever we provoked him to forsake us.

His application was:

1st to those who have present communion with God, *trusted through rich mercy that [it] was then in measure my case,* he exerted such to be very careful of avoiding all he mentioned as causes of God's departure and what even we experimentally found tending to weaken and lower our spiritual frame and to be much in secret prayer.

2[nd] those who have had communion and have lost it, he directed to renew their applications to the L[ord] J[esus] C[hrist] for restitution of his spirit and concluded

3[rd] with an aw[e]ful caution to sinners, who never had God's presence, nor ever were troubled about the want of it, but what he said on this subject was so peculiar to himself that I cannot attempt [to detail] it.

The whole of his discourse was extraordinary and impressive.

---

61. Orig. 'will bring.'

Spent the evening at Mr. Thorpes.[62]

Thursday [12 June] morning rose early, recommended myself to D[ivine] Providence and embarked for Gravesend;[63] had a safe passage though not the pleasantest, the wind blowing very fresh and cold and contrary and the company disagreeable enough. But I trust had something of a warmth at heart, a sense and feeling of spiritual things, which made amends for all. Landed at 9 and walked home. Was engaged in meditation and prayer the greatest part of the way; found all safe and well and that the Divine goodness had been careful of all my concerns in my absence. Praise the Lord, O my soul. Thy daily preserver and benefactor.

My principal business to town this time was to see and hear Mr. Whitefield, that I might judge and speak of him from my own knowledge. From what I have seen in different places of the great work of revival which God has owned under his hand, as well as from the character given of him by several on whose judgment I could well depend, I have long entertained a respect for him, and prayed for a blessing on his endeavours for God's glory. But now I must say, 'Behold, the one half was not told me.'[64] I desire to praise God for these opportunities I have had of hearing, and that in hearing I trust the Lord (who only could do it) opened my heart to attend and profit by him; more especially I would be thankful

---

62. Possibly a relative of a Miss Thorpe with whom he corresponded. Newton published three letters to her in *Cardiphonia* in *Works*, 2:133-139.

63. This town is near the mouth of the Thames and from there he would travel southeast about ten miles by land to Chatham.

64. Quoting 1 Kings 10:7 where the Queen of Sheba expresses her awe at seeing the splendour of Solomon's court.

for that happy communion I shared in Sunday morning. I bless God I am kept from a party spirit, and that I am neither fearful nor desirous of being called after the names of men. But if acknowledging and admiring the manifestation of His grace and providence in the person of Mr. Whitefield should bring me under any kind of reproach, I hope I shall be enabled cheerfully to suffer it for the testimony of a good conscience; to stand up in a spirit of meekness in[65] his vindication, and to remember frequently to pray for a blessing on his public labours and private concernments, that he may stand against all opposition, and always, as hitherto, find his strength proportioned to his day. Amen

The principal intervals of this day have been employed in writing the foregoing. I hope I had some comfort in secret [prayer] this morning and an enlargement in private – something of the frame I had at London is still with me. Lord continue it and suffer neither by my pride or my folly to provoke Thee to depart.

Saturday 14 June I have been walking abroad this evening and summing up the week, in attempting to praise the Lord for all his goodness afforded to me through it, for protecting me from evil, giving me daily bread and especially (as I trust feeding my soul with the bread of life) in the sacrament on Sunday morning and in the plentiful harvest of Gospel ordinances I have been favoured with. It has indeed been a week of continual feasting and privileges for though my frame as it stands in the affections is much lower than it was on Tuesday, yet I hope I still continue to have communion with God in my duties. I find however enough of my own to be humbled for, pride, wanderings, and self-seeking, amiss

---

65. Bull, *Newton*, 73, changed this to *for*.

with my best enjoyments. But there is a fountain opened
for all defilement and to that I hope I have been daily
brought. My person and performances have still need of
continual sprinkling. Glory be to free grace for what is
right; the evil is properly my own. But I trust it is by
imputation laid upon him who has undertaken to bear
it out of God's sight for ever. I have been praying for
a blessing on tomorrow's services, for myself and for
others and that the Lord would magnifie* his power in
owning the dispensations of his faithful ministers, for
the conversion of sinners and the comfort and building
up his children in faith and love. Lord hear and pardon
my imperfect petitions, and let not my weakness prevent my improving though I should sit under inferior
gifts and means, than those I have lately enjoy[ed], let
me look beyond the dispenser and remember that the
work is thine and from Thee and Thee only, I can expect
a blessing.'[66]

[Editor's Note: This ends the full section of Newton's diary for June 6-14]

London Visits Come To An End

The next morning in Chatham he attended the local
Methodist Meeting house and heard Mr. Gibson, whom
Newton described as 'a young preacher and of but indifferent gifts.' For Newton, the sermon was 'a loose unme-
thodical discourse, with many repetitions and tautolo-
gies' that was hard to follow. He admitted, 'the sum and
substance of what he said was gospel truth' but he was
distracted with what was missing. He then confessed his
own error. 'It is my fault and weakness to look so much

---

66. Diary [1]. 6 – 14 June 1755.

upon the instrument, as I generally do. Mr. Whitefield too much captivated me with the power of his preaching; today I fell into the contrary error, and was ready to reject the gold because mingled with dross.' After the service, Newton spent the rest of the afternoon in spiritual conversation with a friend. Part of that conversation as Newton described it was 'chiefly taken up in my declaring what I heard and found from Mr. Whitefield and in communicating experiences.'[67]

Two weeks later he heard Mr. Eades, a Methodist lay preacher. This time Newton was struck with the sermon. 'I think I never heard anything more sweet and impressive.' What especially impressed him was that Eades had little, if any training. 'I adore the grace and providence of God that calls out and supports such persons without learning and without provision, and makes them equal in gifts and success' because they have used 'every probable means' available to them. No doubt this understanding would later influence Newton in his own decisions. And he was becoming less hesitant to associate with Methodists. 'And I would praise him too, that I am not carry'd* away by the sound of a name and that the term of a Methodist preacher does not frighten me from attending upon them, for though I will not give them the preference to other able ministers of the gospel, whom I love and honour, yet if I mistake not, these have been more owned and blessed to me, for the little time I have known them than any.' Therefore, he concluded, 'Happy shall I be if I am accounted worthy to stand near the meanest of these despised persecuted people at the great day. I hope and pray therefore that I may be ena-

---

67. Diary [1], 15 June 1755.

bled chearfully* to bear any part of their reproach now if it should fall upon me for vindicating and admiring them.'[68] Though Newton had clearly aligned himself with White-field's Calvinistic Methodism, he was sympathetic to the Methodists following Wesley.

In the middle of June, Joseph Manesty, who was his former employer in Liverpool, informed Newton that he had successfully recommended Newton for the position as a Tide Surveyor in Liverpool. This was a senior gov-ernment posting in Customs overseeing the harbour. On learning of this offer, Newton prayed about it and sent his letter of consent. Manesty had been assured that Newton's appointment was approved. But unknown to Newton, a dispute soon arose over who should get the position. It was a plum government appointment and once others, including the mayor, heard it was open they lobbied to get their own candidates appointed. Fortu-nately for Newton, Manesty's application was reaffirmed in the end. Consequently, Newton set out alone for Liver-pool in August 1755. He was pleased to have work, espe-cially after almost a year being unemployed. But it meant he had to leave Polly behind in Chatham for a few months because of her poor health. She would rejoin him when she was well enough to travel. On the way, he stopped in London for one last visit to the Sunday services that had meant so much to him: 'morning at the Tabernacle, fore-noon at Mr. Brewers; afternoon, Dr. Jennings.'[69]

This brought an end to his having both leisure and op-portunity to experience the vital evangelical religious life in

---

68. Diary [1], 29 June 1755.

69. Diary [1], 10 Aug. 1755.

London. In the first half of 1755, his diary indicates that he made five visits to London, comprising more than thirteen weeks.[70] Aitken, reviewing this period in Newton's diary, calculated that he went to 'over forty churches, chapels or meeting-houses.'[71] This included often hearing sermons in three different churches or chapels on Sunday, and attending numerous mid-week meetings and lectures.

Bruce Hindmarsh, after examining Newton's activities during this London period, observes that it was 'a steady Calvinistic diet.' He goes on to say, 'If there was a Puritan tradition in London which survived into the eighteenth century, this was it... . Newton would later look back on these heady days in London, when he walked in a cloud of wonder from sermon to sermon, from Church to Chapel to religious society, as the turning point in the settlement of his religious principles.'[72] His reading was in a Calvinistic strain too. In 1754 and 1755, this included Ralph Erskine *Gospel Sonnets*; Thomas Halyburton, *An Extract of the life and death of Mr. Thomas Halyburton*; Matthew Henry, *The Communicants Companion*; James Hervey, *Theron and Aspasio*; and John Owen, *Christologia*.[73] Newton would later fondly look back on his visits to London and comment on them in his autobiography. 'I had likewise access to some religious societies, and became known to many excellent Christians in private. Thus when in London, I lived at the fountain-head, as it were, for spiritual advantages.'[74]

---

70. Hindmarsh, *Newton*, 69. Newton did not write in his diary in the last half of 1754.

71. Aitken, *Newton*, 128.

72. Hindmarsh, *Newton*, 69, 70.

73. For his full reading list, see Hindmarsh, *Newton*, 332-336.

74. Letter 14, *An Authentic Narrative*, 90.

3

Liverpool (1755-1757)

Settling In At Liverpool

On arriving in Liverpool, he found accommodation in a rooming house and settled into his new occupation. This hard-to-obtain government appointment now brought Newton job security, a settled position on land, and an annual salary of £150. One can sense his pride in his new employment and no doubt his relief in having work. This is seen in his letter to Polly, the day after he started. 'I find my duty is to attend the tides one week, and to visit the ships that arrive, and such as are in the river; and the other week to inspect the vessels in the docks, and thus alternately the year round. The latter is little more than a sinecure,[1] but the former requires pretty constant attendance, both by day and by night. I have a good office, with fire and candle, fifty or sixty people under my direction, with a handsome six-oared boat and a coxswain, to row me about in form.'[2] He described his new responsibilities including the risks to John Catlett, Polly's brother.

> Last week I acted as boarding surveyor, that is, going on board ships on their first arrival, some at the rock,

---

1. A position that requires little or no work.
2. *Letters to a Wife*, 20 Aug. 1755, in *Works*, 5:494.

some nearer land. The weather was rough, and there was* a great many fresh arrivals. Being obliged to attend tides by night as well as by day I found myself a little fatigued at the week's end. I have now entered upon my quiet week, which is only to visit and clear the ships on the docks without going into a boat at all and have time enough on my hands.[3]

The Rock (as Newton often wrote it with a capital) mentioned above was a high place of land along the harbour where Newton could look for incoming ships.[4] He describes this to Polly, 'on my first cruise down to the Rock. We saw a vessel, and wandered upon the hills, till she came in. I then went on board, and performed my office with all due gravity.'[5] During inclement weather or low ship traffic, he had time for personal study at his private office at the Weigh-house.

Being permanently stationed in Liverpool, he was now able to be more involved in life in the town. The most important for him now was being part of a local evangelical church. In previous times in Liverpool, even following his conversion, he had gone only to one of the Established churches in town. However, though he would maintain a loose connection with the Established Church, the very first weekend after his arrival, he attended the Baptist church on Stanley Street where John Johnson was the pastor. Johnson (1705/6-1791) had originally been the pastor of Byrom Street Baptist church in Liverpool from about 1741, but his increasingly high Calvinistic

---

3. Newton to John Catlett, quoted in Aitken, *Newton*, 133.

4. A few times he refers to it as 'rock hills' (Diary [1], 18 Aug. 1755).

5. *Letters to a Wife*, 20 Aug. 1755, *Works*, 5:494.

views and tendency for theological hair-splitting caused a church schism.[6] Hence, Johnson and his supporters left about 1747-8 to form a new congregation and opened their new chapel on Stanley Street in 1750.[7] Newton was probably unaware of Johnson's tendencies because he was impressed when he heard him. That first Sunday he said, 'I found my heart warm as he thus skilfully discoursed of the Great truths of the gospel and it was with regret I reflected that through inattention or prejudice I had deprived myself of his preaching for so many years as I have been in town.'[8] Consequently he began attending regularly on Sundays and joined in the mid-week meetings.

Whitefield Preaches In Liverpool

Unexpectedly, just as he was settling into the schedule of work and worship, the next month his routine was suddenly interrupted. He was about to enjoy a special privilege that was greater than what he had experienced in London. George Whitefield came to town. We now return to Newton's complete diary notes that cover Whitefield's first and only planned preaching visit to Liverpool.[9] Providentially, Whitefield arrived when Newton was on his quiet week at the docks, rather than out in the harbour. Hence, Newton had time to hear and connect with Whitefield. Fortunately for readers today, in contrast to when he heard Whitefield

---

6. J. H.Y. Briggs, 'Johnson, John, (1706-1791)', *DEB*, 612; Cecil/Rouse, *Newton*, 302.

7. S. L. Copson, 'Johnson, John (1705/6–1791)', *Oxford Dictionary of National Biography*, Oxford University Press, 2004 ‹http://www. oxforddnb.com/view/article/14894 ›[accessed 17 Jan 2014].

8. Diary [1], 17 Aug. 1755.

9. Diary [1], 10-15 Sept. 1755.

in London, Newton now had time to include more detailed notes of Whitefield's sermons, and record his personal reflections on them. The following is Newton's complete diary for 10–15 Sept. 1755.

> 'Wednesday 10th Sept...In the evening I went to Mr. Johnson's to joyn* the conference, but heard that Mr. Whitefield was in town and preaching. Went to the W[esleyan] M[eeting] and found he [Whitefield] was about half through his discourse; his text I perceived was our Lord's question to Peter and his answer, John 21:17,

[SERMON 7]

> [17He saith unto him the third time, Simon, son of Jonas, lovest thou me? Peter was grieved because he said unto him the third time, Lovest thou me? And he said unto him, Lord, thou knowest all things; thou knowest that I love thee. Jesus saith unto him, Feed my sheep.]

> from which he was giving the evidences of a true love to Christ. The following he mentioned after I came in:

>> union and communion - the one the cause; the other the effect,
>> a delight in real holiness,
>> a hatred of sin,
>> a love to all his people, ways and ordinances,
>> a heart raised above the world,
>> and a desire and waiting for his gracious appearance.

> *With all these I hope my heart has some acquaintance and that my soul does in these senses love the Lord (alas that I love him so*

little). From this he inferred comfort to the believer, in God's everlasting love, for this is the cause of his having drawn us to love in time. He concluded with a very solemn warning and offer to sinners.

Thursday 11th Sept. rose about ½ past 4. Mr. Whitfield* preached at 5 from **Isaiah 25:4**

[SERMON 8]

[⁴For thou hast been a strength to the poor, a strength to the needy in his distress, a refuge from the storm, a shadow from the heat, when the blast of the terrible ones is as a storm against the wall.]

a refuge from the storm and shewed* how Christ was a sure and compleat* defence from all the storms to which we are liable;

> from the storm of the guilt,
>
> the storm of the power of sin,
>
> the storm of affliction,
>
> of temptation,
>
> the stormy blast of death,
>
> and the heavy storm of God's eternal wrath which is denounced against transgressors.

I can only mention some of the heads. The power and substance of his discourses are not to be wrote* by me; When he applyed* himself to congratulate believers on their security against these formidable evils, my heart rejoyced* in hope and when he applyed* to sinners it seemed impossible any should stand out. But the experience shews* that unless the Lord in a powerful manner interposes, vain are the best preachers. Though an angel was to descend from glory, he could make no converts but where God opens the heart.

In the afternoon, visited him and had 2 hours close conversation with great comfort and satisfaction. When I went [to go] away he invited to sup with him, which I did.

[SERMON 9]

He preached at 6 from **Heb. 2: 3**.

[**³How shall we escape, if we neglect so great salvation; which at the first began to be spoken by the Lord, and was confirmed unto us by them that heard him.**]

He shewed*:

First, the greatness of the salvation in the Gospel.

1st great with respect to its author - the Lord Jesus;

2nd great in the extent of it reaching to all sins, all nations and all ages.

3rd great in the price for it - the blood of Christ.

4th great in the blessed effects in deliverance from sin and hell.

5th great in its privileges here and hereafter.

Secondly, our extreme danger if we neglect this salvation. 'How shall we escape?' This he enlarged upon in his usual way of application.

Friday, 12 September. I find my frame rising* again, something in the same way as when I heard Mr. W[hitefield] at London though in an inferior degree. Rose early and engaged in prayer with more composure

than common till 5; particularly I prayed that this blessing the Lord has now sent the town may not be in vain.
Then went to the meeting. Mr.W[hitefield] preached
from **John 6:35**

[SERMON 10]

[³⁵ And Jesus said unto them, I am the bread of life:
he that cometh to me shall never hunger; and he that
believeth on me shall never thirst.]

and shewed*:

> in what senses Christ is the bread of life,
>
> who they are that properly come to him and believe
> on him,
>
> and how it is that they shall never hunger or thirst
> more.

A warm experimental discourse¹⁰ which cheared my poor cold
heart. I was led to see that I do through grace feed upon Christ in
my heart by faith with thanksgiving, that the Lord has brought me
willingly to Christ and enabled me to believe on him; and that in
consequence thereof, my hunger and thirst after this world and its
vanities are abated. I find something of a sweet satisfaction where
before there was a void and emptiness. And that [the] hunger and
thirst which I trust I now principally feel, is after righteousness,
and that spiritual meat and drink, with which thou hast promised
to nourish us here and to satisfy us abundantly hereafter.*

Dined with Mr. W[hitefield] at Mr. Fisher's.¹¹ Who am
I thus to be admitted into such company and yet what is

---

10. This is a discourse that applies the biblical text to the experience
of the listeners so as to impact their lives.

11. Full name added by Rouse in Cecil/Rouse, *Newton*, 93.

this to the hope of admission into full communion with the saints in light.

In the evening, he preached from these words 'I am the way' John 14:6.

[SERMON 11]

[⁶Jesus saith unto him, I am the way, the truth, and the life: no man cometh unto the Father, but by me.]

After a very engaging introduction, he spoke of the several senses in which Christ is the way of his people.

1ˢᵗ he is the way to pardon.

2ⁿᵈ to righteousness.

3ʳᵈ to sanctification.

4ᵗʰ he is the way as our intercessor, through whom alone we have access to God in all these things, he is our way and our only way.

5ᵗʰ he is the way as our example and if we really abide in him, we must in our measure walk even as he walked.

He then applyed* the word:

1ˢᵗ to such as were at present in this way, stirring them up to more diligence therein.

2ⁿᵈ to backsliders from the way.

3ʳᵈ to such as were as yet walking in ways of their own.

There was a numerous congregation, vastly attentive and I hope signs of a beginning work; [may] the Lord increase and carry it on. Amen.

[Later that evening, Newton eagerly wrote to Polly to share the events.

'Most of my leisure this week will be taken up with Mr. Wh[itfiel]d, which, as it is an occasional interruption, and from which I hope both for comfort and benefit, I think you will excuse. He came to town on Wednesday, preached on that evening, twice yesterday, and so will continue preaching twice a day while he stays. We shall try to keep him till Monday; though he says he never was in a place where he had so little encouragement to stay as here.

I made myself known to him the first night; went to see him, and conversed with him the next morning, when he invited me to supper. I went home with him from the preaching, and stayed till ten o'clock. So we are now very great;[12] and very thankful I would be for the privilege. May the Lord yet give him to see, that his labour of love among us is not in vain! But surely this is the most unconcerned town, for its size, in the kingdom. I hope he is sent to awaken some of the people out of their false peace. However he is, as he was formerly, very helpful to me. He warms my heart, makes me more indifferent to cares and crosses, and strengthens my faith.'[13]]

Saturday 13 September. Rose as yesterday in a comfortable frame; prayed for a blessing upon the preaching to myself and to others and I hope was answered for both. My own heart was greatly affected and there seemed to be concern upon many of the hearers. His text was **Rev. 3:20**.

---

12. Close, intimate, much acquainted (Johnson, *Dictionary*, 1768; Hindmarsh, *Newton*, 73).

13. *Letters to a Wife*, 12 Sept. 1755 in *Works* 5: 502, 503.

[SERMON 12]

[²⁰Behold, I stand at the door, and knock: if any man hear my voice, and open the door, I will come in to him, and will sup with him, and he with me.]

He began with observing from the context, the hatefulness and danger of a lukewarm spirit in religion. He divided the words as they lye*, speaking:

1ˢᵗ of the person – 'behold I' – the Lord Jesus himself.

2ⁿᵈ the action – 'I stand at the door and knock.'

3ʳᵈ the extent – 'if any man hear my voice and open.' He cleared this from a free will sense. God knocks at the door of our hearts by his providence both in afflictions and blessings. But it is he only can open the heart and procure himself admission. Yet as he does this by sweetly leading our own wills to receive him, in great condescension he is pleased to speak of it and to reward it, as if was our own act and deed.

4[th]the promise– 'I will come into him and sup,' etc. Under this he illustrated a most beautiful experience, shewing* how we sup; that is how we have communion with God in secret prayer, in reading the word, in meditation, in public worship and in the ordinance of the Lord's supper peculiarly so called.

He applyed* the raising of Lazarus in this view. Like him, we are dead in trespasses. We stink and are an offence before God. We are bound with our corruptions as he with grave cloths and a stone, heavier than that which was laid on his tomb, lies hard upon our hearts. But the Lord by his power removes this stone. He calls us by his word; though dead, we hear the voice of God and live. He frees us from our bands and impediments, and to crown all, he makes us [sit] down with him and feasts [with] us at his own table. He not only sups with us but we with him.

Surely, the Lord opened my heart; at this time the tears run down my eyes with joy, that I could understand and through grace have experienced something of these divine things. Many as I said seemed much moved. He divided his application as usual so that everyone had something. I hope it was and will be made a happy opportunity to many. Praise the Lord, O my soul.

In the evening he preached from **Eph. 5:14** 'Awake thou that sleepest.'

[SERMON 13]

[**14Wherefore he saith, Awake thou that sleepest, and arise from the dead, and Christ shall give thee light.**]

[He] shewed* the sense of the word *sleep* as it refers to the unregenerate and to believers. In like manner the meaning of *awake*, he beautifully illustrated [with] the parable of the prodigal and the account of Peter's denial and repentance.

A warm and striking discourse and the meeting [was] as full as it could hold.

Afterwards I went home and sup'd with him; returned and went to bed in peace, after prayers, etc. suitable to the close of another week enriched with so many mercies and priviledges*. Alass*, how unsuitable I should rather say.14

---

14. Newton clearly wrote *unsuitable*. One 18th century alternative meaning of this word is *not proportionate*. If that is his meaning here, he is saying that the great blessings he received through Whitefield's preaching and fellowship (Wed.-Sat.) were out of proportion to the days earlier in his week.

Sunday, 14ᵗʰ September. Rose early, spent an hour in prayer, etc. then walked till the time of Mr. Whitefield's preaching. His text was **Col. 3:4**.

[SERMON 14]

[⁴When Christ, who is our life, shall appear, then shall ye also appear with him in glory.]

He shewed:*

  1ˢᵗ in what senses Christ is our life.

  2ⁿᵈ how he shall appear.

  3ʳᵈ the certainty and manner of our appearing with him.

In the experimental part of his discourse, I think it may be said in a limited sense that he opened the kingdom of heaven to all believers, such displays of glory, such supports against worldly tryals* and temptations – but I cannot repeat them. His application to sinners was aw[e]ful, yet encouraging.

In the forenoon, I waited upon him to St. Thomas's Church¹⁵ and had I believe the honour of being pointed at this day upon several occasions as one of his followers; especially as he was so obliging to go home with me and dine with me. He heard the preacher, the very reverse of himself: no life in his delivery, no gospel in his discourse. After dinner, I waited on him home and then went to Mr. Johnson's. Heard an exceeding good

---

15. St. Thomas's Church, on Park Lane, was consecrated in 1750 and was known for its 216-foot slender tower (W. Reginald Ward and Richard P. Heitzenrater, eds., *The Works of John Wesley* (Nashville, Tenn., 1992), 21:94, n64.

discourse from Jer. 30:21 latter [part] setting forth the sufficiency and glory of Christ in all his relations and offices and the security and peace his people may find therein.

At 5, Mr. Whitefield preached in St. Thomas Square to an audience of perhaps 4,000, from **Rom. 13:14**.

[SERMON 15]

[¹⁴But put ye on the Lord Jesus Christ, and make not provision for the flesh, to fulfil the lusts thereof.]

First part he shewed*

    1st what was not putting on Christ:

        not an attachment to partys* or professions,
        not a stated attendance upon ordinances,
        not a course of moral performances.

    2nd he shewed* what it was:

        that is to receive Christ in the heart as a principle of sanctification.
        and to be clothed with his imputed righteousness as the only ground of our justification.

He applyed* these things both to saints and sinners. I trust many were edified and quickened and some convinced. I spent the evening with him at his lodging, and returned home in a sweet and composed frame.

Monday, 15 September. Rose early and waited upon Mr. Whitefield a little way out of town, when at length we were forced to part. My heart and prayers [are] with him. Continued walking about an hour. In the forenoon went to the Rock, engaged at times in comforting the afflicted Mr. Flemming,[16] but the Lord alone can comfort in such a case; Lord, why not me.

Through the whole of this day, I have had a sense of God's presence, and a desire to walk with him in everything. O that this may be my habitual temper.'[17]

This ends Newton's full diary notes covering Whitefield's visit to Liverpool.

In a letter to Lady Huntingdon, Whitefield gave his impression of this visit. 'The only new ground that has been broken up is Liverpool. There the prospect is promising. I preached in a great square on the Lord's-day and the alarm I hear went through the town.'[18] Whitefield considered Liverpool new ground for him because he had preached there only once, two years earlier. Of that brief earlier visit, Whitefield wrote: 'A person, who had been wrought on by some of my printed sermons, met me at landing, and took me to his house. A great number, at a short notice, were convened; all were quiet; and some came under immediate conviction.' [19]

---

16. Newton described this in his letter to Polly, Sept. 16. 'I commenced acquaintance yesterday with a good man, who lately lost his wife in child-bed the first year. He is the very picture of sorrow. I attempt to comfort him, though I succeed but poorly. It is only God who can give comfort in such a case. Yet I think few can be more capable of sympathising with him than myself. What I have lately gone through is fresh upon my mind' (*Works*, 5:504). Because Newton had nearly lost his beloved Polly, he could empathise with him.

17. Diary [1]. 10 – 15 Sept. 1755.

18. Whitefield to Lady Huntingdon, 24 Sept. 1755 quoted in Tyerman, *Whitefield*, 2:352.

19. Whitefield to ___, 27 Oct. 1753, Tyerman, *Whitefield*, 2:316n. Tyerman, incorrectly guessed that the Liverpool greeter was probably Newton. Newton was not there in 1753.

The next day Newton enthusiastically provided Polly, who was still in Chatham, with his summary of what had happened during Whitefield's visit. 'Mr. Wh[itefiel]d left us yesterday morning; I accompanied him on foot a little way out of town, till the chaise overtook us. I have had more of his company than would have come to my share at London in a twelvemonth. I heard him preach nine times, supped with him three times, and dined with him once at Mr. F[isher]'s, and on Sunday, he dined with me.' Newton expressed his deep admiration for Whitefield and his impact on the town. 'I cannot say how much I esteem him, and hope, to my dying day, I shall have reason to bless God in his behalf. Having never been here before but one night, he was not known or regarded by the fashionable folks, though several of them went to hear him. But many of the poorer sort are inquiring after him with tears.'[20]

A week later, Newton was still humming with excitement from Whitefield's visit so he gave Polly further details about Whitefield dining with him. He informs her that when he first invited his landlady to hear Whitefield, she could hardly give him a civil answer, 'though otherwise she is very obliging and respectful.' Newton continues, 'But curiosity, or a better motive, prevailing, she went on the second day. She returned very well disposed; and asked me if I had any of his printed sermons. I lent her a volume. She went to hear him again, and became his great admirer.' As a result, 'She herself first proposed my asking him to dinner; and his behaviour there, confirmed her in her respect for him. I invited four or five Christian friends to partake of his company. She provided

---

20. *Letters to a Wife*, 16 Sept. 1755 in *Works* 5: 503, 504.

a handsome dinner, and when I spoke of the additional expense, she said she was very willing to bear it; but I do not intend that she shall.' Consequently, 'She has borne the reproach and laugh of many of her neighbours very well. They call her a Methodist, and she seems as easy under the charge as I am. So, we see, very unlikely things may be brought about.'[21]

Newton's close association with Whitefield during that visit drew derogatory jibes from those who did not look kindly upon Whitefield's ministry. He shared this with Polly. 'I go on making useful acquaintance. The Lord honours me in the eyes of his own people, which is the honour I most desire. And though some of the wags of my acquaintance have given me the name of young White-field, from my constant attendance upon him when he was here.' Yet of this he reflected, 'it does not grieve me; and perhaps, if they would speak the truth, they do not think the worse of me in their hearts. I find I cannot be consistent and conscientious in my profession, without incurring the charge of singularity[22]. I shall endeavour to act with prudence, and not give needless offence; but I hope I shall never more be ashamed of the Gospel.'[23] He had come to accept the inevitable cost of aligning himself with the revivalist, and those like him.

Finding a Church Home but Burdened For the Town

The Sunday after Whitefield left town, Newton returned to the Methodist Meeting. However, because he had

---

21. *Letters to a Wife*, 26 Sept. 1755 in *Works* 5: 507.

22. Odd or peculiar.

23. *Letters to a Wife*, 23 Sept. 1755 in *Works* 5: 506.

worked on the tides till midnight, he woke up late and had to run to the meeting. No doubt he was hoping to continue to experience that he had when Whitefield was there. But he lamented, 'I had perhaps staid* at home; a poor confused inconsistent discourse.'[24] However, he admitted it was not all the preacher's fault because he could hardly keep himself awake. Later that morning he went for the first time to hear John Oulton (d. 1780), the pastor at Byrom Street Baptist church. This was the church that Johnson had left to form Stanley Street Baptist church, seven years earlier. Oulton came to Byrom Street right after this split and served as pastor till 1765. Newton admitted he would not have gone to hear him 'but that Mr. Whitefield recommended him as an excellent humble man.'[25]

Oulton is not well known so details must be gleaned from a variety of sources. Before coming to Liverpool, he was pastor of the Baptist church (1731-1748) in Leominster. His son, also called John, attended Bristol Baptist Academy, a well-respected training school for pastors. Just a month before meeting Newton, Oulton had preached at the ordination of his son who became pastor of the Baptist church in Rawdon.[26] Oulton was a supporter of the Evangelical Revival. He corresponded with Howell Harris who described him as 'the only

---

24. Diary [1], Sunday, 21 Sept. 1755.

25. Diary [1], 21 Sept. 1755.

26. Roger Hayden, *Continuity and Change: Evangelical Calvinism among eighteenth-century Baptist Ministers Trained at Bristol Academy, 1690-1791* (Oxfordshire, 2006), 239; J.M., 'History of the Baptist Church at Rawdon,' *Baptist Magazine* (1818), 10:458,459.

Baptist to be clear of bigotry.'[27] Oulton attended the first Society of Ministers arranged by Harris near Brecon, Wales, 1 October 1740, which today is about forty-five miles from Leominster.[28] There is record of Oulton corresponding with Whitefield and Wesley as early as 1739. He wrote a letter of encouragement to John Wesley. 'You know well that tall cedars are far more exposed in a storm, than low shrubs. The more successful you are against Satan's kingdom, the more likely you are to be the butt of his rage and malice... . Yet, I trust that you live in that Spirit [who will] ... secure you from all Satan's strong delusions, which is my heart's desire and fervent prayer to God for you.'[29] But when that year Wesley circulated his controversial sermon *Free Grace*, Oulton published a forty-eight page response entitled *A Vindication of the Seventeenth Article of the Church of England, from the Aspersions*

---

27. Howell Harris to George Whitefield, 30 April 1742, in Boyd Stanley Schlenther and Eryn Mant White, *Calendar of the Trevecka Letters* (Aberystwyth, Wales, 2003), 82. There are fifteen extant letters between Oulton and Harris, 1740-1745, listed in this *Calendar*.

28. Geraint Tudur in Robert Pope, ed., *Honouring the Past and Shaping the Future: Religious and Biblical Studies in* Wales (Leominster, Herefordshire, 2003), 135.

29. John Oulton to John Wesley, 13 July 1739, *Supplement to the Arminian Magazine* (1797), 25, 26. Oulton also mentions receiving a letter from Whitefield. Wesley records that he wrote to Oulton on 9 July, 28 July and 7 October. See Ward and Heitzenrater, *Works of John Wesley*, 19:397, 400, 436.

cast on it in a Sermon lately published by Mr. John Wesley.[30]
Oulton explains to the readers that he had habit to
'heartily pray for the influences he [God] pleases to make
use of, and wish them abundant success. Such was* my
hopes concerning this gentleman.' He continues, however
'the frequent reports of the manner of his attacking an
express* doctrine of Christ, and the reformation, I was
unwilling to believe, till I saw it in print.'[31] Oulton,
though a Baptist, takes the interesting tack of defending
Article seventeen of the Established Church which is
entitled 'Of Predestination and Election.' He points out
that Wesley, who was still in the Established Church,
was teaching something contrary to its doctrine. When
Howell Harris read Oulton's *Vindication*, he thought it
was 'excellent' and urged Whitefield to 'recommend to
everyone.'[32] In April 1742 Oulton invited Whitefield to
preach in Leominster. In response, Whitefield wrote that
he was committed elsewhere but would come as soon as

---

30. This does not include his seven-page pastoral letter, at the beginning, to the readers whom he addresses 'dearly beloved.' The
printed date on Oulton's *Vindication* is MDCCLX [1760]. This
is an error because the title says 'sermon *lately* published (ital-
ics added) but Oulton is clearly addressing Wesley's published
sermon of 1739 and his quotes from Wesley's sermon, including
pagination, match that sermon published in 1739. For example
see *Vindication*, 19, 20. Originals of both can be found online in
Gale Eighteenth-Century Collections Online (ECCO).

31. Oulton, *Vindication*, 3, 4.

32. Howell Harris to George Whitefield, 29 March 1741, in Schlenther and White, *Trevecka Letters*, 321. Harris gives the full title of
Oulton's *Vindication* so this confirms that the date of MDCCLX
in the printed *Vindication* is wrong. Possibly it was MDCCXL
(1740).

he could. He included a word of exhortation. 'My dear
brother, I rejoice to hear you are helped in your work.
Let this encourage you; go on, go on; the more we do, the
more we may do for Jesus'[33] They wrote again to each
other in May. The work under Oulton was beginning to
bear fruit and Whitefield encouraged him further. 'May
he use and bless you ever more and more.' [34] The next
year Whitefield came to Leominster on 27 April where he
preached twice. Of that visit he declared that 'the Lord
broke up the fallow ground.'[35]

Newton's first impression of Oulton was that he spoke
'sweetly' on John 15 but in contrast to Johnson he was
'not perhaps so deep in delivering the doctrines.' However, Oulton had an advantage. 'I dare say he is a sound and
experimental[36] preacher,' wrote Newton, 'and deals more
in application than the other [Johnson] which I have always found the most useful to me.' Hence, Newton rejoiced, 'I have the privilege of two gospel ministers where
I expected there were none. The Lord grant they may be
[a source of] blessings to me.'[37] That afternoon, he heard
Johnson twice. The following day he visited Oulton and
'had much satisfaction in his converse.' On leaving, Oulton invited him to come along to visit the home of one of

---

33. Whitefield to Oulton, (6 April 1742) in George Whitefield, *Letters
of George Whitefield, for the Period 1734-1742* (Edinburgh; Carlisle reprint 1976; reprint vol. 1 of *Whitefield's Works*, 1771, plus additional
letters), 381, 382.

34. Whitefield to Oulton, (27 May 1742) in Whitefield, *Letters of
George Whitefield (1976)*, 393, 394.

35. Tyerman, *Whitefield*, 2:59.

36. Applies the text to the experience of the believer.

37. Diary [1], 21 Sept. 1755.

his members. He accepted and was very encouraged by the visit. 'I was more pleased with these, as they seem to enjoy a catholic free spirit and are not bound up within the limits of a party as some here and too many every-where are.'[38] The next Sunday afternoon he went again to hear Oulton. After, he met with Oulton who loaned him a book of Erskine's sermons and provided pastoral care. 'Mr. Oulton prayed for me and my dear [Polly who was ill in Chatham] in a very affectionate manner which touched my heart.'[39] From then on, Newton often went to Sunday meetings at both churches, but soon New-ton chose to stop attending Johnson's mid-week society meetings and instead joined those at Oulton's.[40] He also regularly squeezed in attending the Methodist chapel, as well as the Established Church for the sacrament.

All this was very satisfying but over the next four months he became increasingly concerned about the gen-eral low spiritual condition of the town and of many of its churches and chapels. Consequently, he wrote to White-field and pled for him to return. The full letter follows.

Rev. and Dear Sir,

The permission you gave me to write was so agreeable to me that I am surprized* at myself for putting it off so long. One cause indeed of my waiting was in hopes of giving you some of the particulars of the good effects of your late preaching amongst us. There were many en-quirers after you, the week you left town and many were greatly disappointed and grieved to hear you were gone.

---

38. Diary [1], 22 Sept. 1755.

39. Diary [1], 28 Sept. 1755.

40. Hindmarsh, *Newton*, 77.

But as those they spoke to, neglected to ask [for] their names or circumstances, I can only say in general that there is great reason to hope your labour of love has not been in vain, without being able to assign any particular instances. I hope it will please the Lord to give you opportunity and direction to visit us again soon, and I shall take it as a happy earnest that he is about to come amongst us in the power of his Spirit, that he sends his faithful messengers before him.

The low estate of the gospel in this very populous town has, I doubt not, excited your wonder and compassion, and was I acquainted with every spiritual minister in the land methinks I would address them all in the same way *Come over hither and help us.* Here are more than forty thousand people, who in matters of religion hardly know their right hand from their left, people that are destroyed for lack of knowledge,[41] or by unskilful, corrupt teachers. Here the tenets of the Arians and Socinians[42] are not only held, but propagated with the most pernicious address; the satisfaction and divinity of the blessed Jesus slighted and degraded even by those who call themselves his ministers. Here is such a departure from God as is indeed grievous to behold. Profaneness and insensibility seem to divide all between them, and a flow of outward prosperity has blinded all ranks, orders and degrees. Are not these strong motives to engage such ministers as have the cause of God and the good of souls at heart (and who would take a peculiar pleasure to own their Master's name where it is the least held in esteem) to Liverpool? Their zeal, their compassion, their faith and their patience will all find abundant exercise. Our Lord has said 'wherever the carcass is there will the eagles be gathered together.'[43]

---

41. Hosea 4:6.

42. Both of these deny the full deity of Christ.

43. Matt. 24:28. The King James refers to eagles but many newer translations change this to *vultures.*

It is with pleasure I hear of a work of revival going on in so many different parts of the kingdom; and, as an inhabitant of this town, I am grieved to think that we should be as yet excluded from a share in it.

It is true, we have the truth preached in the Baptist meetings; but I believe you know the particular disadvantages they are both under, so that, though they are useful to their own people (I trust, through grace, to me also), yet they seem not calculated for general usefulness. The unhappy bigotry of Mr. Wesley's people here is another great disadvantage to the cause. They have the best house in the place, yet they will neither suffer any but their own people to preach in it, nor will they keep it supplied themselves. I have been quite pained and ashamed to see what empty ignorant pretenders have undertaken to speak to the people, in the name of God, at that place.

I beg dear sir, you will bear us in mind, perhaps Providence may show you a way of assisting us. At least, I hope you will pray for us and in good time appear among us again, your setting your hand to the work a second time may have an effect beyond all our expectations, it may revive old convictions, raise new ones and if you favour us with a timely notice of your intention, I dare promise you a crowded audience at the very first. I apprehend it would be of great service if you could lay your affairs so as to stay a week amongst us, and procure some other minister either to come with you or follow immediately after, while the people's [hearts] are still warm, to go on where you leave off. If Mr. Adams,[44]

---

44. Thomas Adams, one of Whitefield's preachers and assistants (Dallimore, 2:287, 349). Newton heard him preach at the Tabernacle (Diary [1] 23 March 1755) and commented it was 'a very comfortable sermon.' Bull, *Newton*, p. 68n says he was a minister at the Tabernacle in Rodborough.

Mr. Kinsman,[45] Mr. Middleton[46] (I mention them because I only know them) were to stay here a little while I doubt not but many would be reached, and Mr. Oulton would I dare say lend his meeting, if Mr. Wesley's could not be obtained.[47]

I think I have heard you say you were cautious of introducing a division amongst the Methodists; but I beg to consider that they [who][48] bear that name amongst us [are] very few in number, low for the most part in experience, still lower in knowledge and chiefly distinguished by an ignorant, bigoted zeal and as they go on there is no likelihood of their being either more numerous or more exemplary; and shall 30 or 40 such, keep out an opportunity of declaring the grace of God to thousands? I hope not!

45. Andrew Kinsman (1725-1793) frequently preached at the Moorfields Tabernacle (Dallimore, 2:417). He was converted under the ministry of Whitefield and became the minister of the Plymouth Tabernacle. See Edwin Welch, 'Andrew Kinsman's Churches at Plymouth,' *Report of the Transactions of the Devonshire Association for the Advancement of Science, Literature and Art*, 97 (1965), 212-236 mentioned in Haykin, *The Revived Puritan*, 189n.

46. Middleton whom Whitefield described as 'my dear fellow-labourer' died Sept. 1768 (Tyerman, *Whitefield*, 2:556). Whitefield preached the funeral sermon, entitled 'The furnace of Affliction' based on Isaiah 48:10. Unknown to Whitefield, Joseph Gurney took it down in shorthand and later published it.

47. It is significant that Newton did not include Johnson's church; for he knew Johnson would not be receptive.

48. Orig. they are that bear.

However, till something can be done, I wish you would represent some part of what I have written,[49]to Mr. Wesley, to set before him the importance of this great town, and urge him to send such preachers here (if none may be admitted but of his sending) as [have] skill to divide the word of truth[50]in a lively, affecting manner, and may dwell upon the great essentials of the gospel in the first place, to inform the people of the truths in which all renewed Christians agree, before they puzzle them with the points on which we differ.

I have written[51] with a freedom perhaps not quite suitable to the great respect I have for you, but I hope you will excuse me and believe I mean well.

To close with a word about myself. The time you were[52] down [here] was a harvest season with me. The Lord enlarged my heart to hear His word from your mouth, and I continued for about a week after in a frame beyond my common attainment. But, for the most part since, I have been in the valley, dull, contracted, and unuseful. But, as through Divine grace, I have been led to live above and beyond my frames, upon the everlasting righteousness of my dear Redeemer, to which my best obedience can add no value, and from which all my infirmities can take nothing away. So these things, though they take from my

---

49. Orig., wrote. Newton inserted a comma after *wrote* and before *to Mr. Wesley*. This comma indicates a break in the sentence and would hence mean, 'I wish you would represent to Mr. Wesley some part of what I have written in this letter to you.' Bull, *Newton*, 84 when quoting this part of the letter did not include the comma, hence giving the misleading interpretation. Martin, *Newton*, 176, by not noticing this comma, wrongly says that Newton wrote first to Wesley and later to Whitefield.

50. 2 Timothy 2:15

51. Orig., wrote.

52. Orig. was.

pleasure, have no considerable effect upon my peace. [My path is]⁵³ sometimes miry, dark and heavy which makes me go [at a slow pace]⁵⁴ but I have an infallible guide and his word assures [me that my]⁵⁵ journey's end shall be everlasting rest, light and joy. Therefore, though I have not yet attained, I am still pressing on;⁵⁶ though my infirmities often prevail, I am still strengthened to rally; though I am often cast [down], yet, blessed be God, not yet destroyed⁵⁷ and I trust never shall for the covenant is everlasting and sure. I beg your prayers that I may be kept from scandalising my profession by a careless walk and that I may be endued with a spirit of humility.

I [include my]⁵⁸ earnest prayers that the Lord may go on to bless you and multitudes [through]⁵⁹you and may your latter end [be]more than your beginning.⁶⁰

Believe me to be with a most sincere regard,

Reverend and dear Sir.

Your most affectionate, though unworthy servant and follower in the Lord Jesus.

John Newton

Liverpoole*, the 2ⁿᵈ January 1756

---

53. Words are missing caused by paper tear, but suggested by editor.

54. Words are missing caused by paper tear, but suggested by editor.

55. Words are missing caused by paper tear, but suggested by editor.

56. Philippians 3:10-14.

57. 2 Corinthians 2:9.

58. Words are missing caused by paper tear, but suggested by editor.

59. Words are missing caused by paper tear, but suggested by editor.

60. Allusion to Job 42:12 'So the LORD blessed the latter end of Job more than his beginning.'

[PS] I should greatly esteem the favour of a few lines, which some leisure moment offers.

Please direct to me as Surveyor of the Customs.[61]

It appears that Whitefield responded and indicated he would return. By this time Polly had arrived and they had moved into their own home on Edmund Street, off Old Hall Street.[62] This was just a few blocks from the harbour and near the centre of the town. No doubt, he looked forward to introducing Polly to Whitefield and hosting him in their home. In April he wrote again to Whitefield.[63] The contents of the letter are not known, but it probably repeated his plea for Whitefield to return. But six months later, he received the sad news that Whitefield could not come. Newton recorded his disappointment in his diary: 'Had a letter today from dear Mr. Whitefield, dated at Manchester, after all his purposes and our expectations, I find we must not see him this year. He says there have been golden seasons where he has been northwards for some months at which I sincerely rejoyce.*' Understandably, Newton expressed his sadness and burden for Liverpool. 'But alass* for this poor place. I think it is like what I find [in] Acts 16:6,7[64]

---

61. Newton to Whitefield, 2 Jan. 1756, MS 2935 (ff. 232, 233) at Lambeth Palace.

62. Aitken, *Newton*, 140. One of the present walking tours in Liverpool says the address was 33 Edmund Street.

63. Diary [1] 16 April 1756.

64. 'Now when they had gone throughout Phrygia and the region of Galatia, and were forbidden of the Holy Ghost to preach the word in Asia. After they were come to Mysia, they assayed to go into Bithynia: but the Spirit suffered them not.'

– those who would come over and help us are not permitted. Lord when, when shall our time come?'[65]

Whitefield did not return till eleven years later, after Newton had moved from Liverpool.[66] It is not known if, as Newton requested in January 1756, Whitefield informed Wesley about the spiritual needs in the town. In any case, a year later, John Wesley came to Liverpool in 1757 and this provided Newton's first opportunity to hear him. Newton admitted that he went with some prejudice. But at the end of Wesley's mission in the town, Newton expressed his thanks. 'I desire to bless God on his behalf that I have seen him and heard him. The word has, I hope, done me good by his ministry and the remaining power of bigotry in me has received a blow which (I would hope) will keep it low hereafter.'[67] 'I would hope,' he continued, ' that since the Lord has taken so gracious and favourable a way to correct my ignorance and presumption I shall no more presume[68] to censure and judge without hearing, or dare confine the Spirit of the Lord to those only who tally in all things with my sentiments.' [69]

---

65. Diary [2] Tuesday 19 October 1756.

66. Gillies, *Whitefield Works*, 3:353.

67. Bull, *Newton*, incorrectly transcribed this 'keep *me* low hereafter,' p. 93.

68. Bull, *Newton*, incorrectly transcribed this *venture*, p. 93.

69. Diary [2] 2 May 1757.

4

Liverpool (1757-1764)

A Growing Sense of a Call to Pastoral Ministry
Near the end of 1757, Newton was having an increasing desire to go into pastoral ministry in the Established Church. He was experiencing positive results from his spiritual conversations and several friends had encouraged him to consider becoming a pastor. However, he was well aware that, knowing his own heart, he could easily be deceived and entertain it for the wrong reasons. On the first day of the next year, he reflected on the previous year and his present situation. He had become more dissatisfied with what he experienced in the Established Church. He admitted that now about the only time he attended was for the sacrament. 'When I do go,' he complained, 'there so little of the gospel in the discourses and so little appearance of the power godliness in the audience that everything I see or hear has rather a tendency to damp my devotion, than to raise it.' He thought back to his time in London, three years earlier, and confessed that he had depended too much on others for his spiritual vitality and growth. 'I was apt to idolise means and ministers as tho* they had a power of doing me good of themselves.' He realised that he was part of the problem. Therefore, he committed himself to pray for the town and to be more fervent in his own life. Understandably,

he longed to be among Christians who were vibrant and consistent in their faith and walk. And more than that, he wanted to be part of the solution. 'I particularly surrendered myself to the Lord ... professing my desire both to serve him and to wait his direction, when and how.'[1]

Ministry was on his mind, but he was somewhat confused and in some doubt. 'At present I am under fluctuating doubt, not knowing whether the views I have of late aspired to are the motions of his gracious Spirit, or the fruits of self-will and sufficiency. I should hope they are rather from the former, but that unbelief creeps in with "How can these things be?" How can I be made fit for such a work? Fit at present I certainly am not.' Yet his hope was in God. 'I am an empty vessel which the Lord can fill in a moment.' Therefore, he dedicated himself to seek God's direction. 'I commit myself to the Lord, who will one way or other determine for me in the course of the year'[2] He had begun studying Greek and Hebrew just in case he would be called. He was pleased to record that he could translate a chapter in either Testament without consulting other translations or lexicons. Of course, he was well aware that he needed more than this to be ordained in the Established Church. 'Tho* there is something vastly more important which I must need, but this must come from on high and if the Lord delight in me for his service it will not be withheld.'[3]

For more satisfying Christian fellowship and ministry from the pulpit, he continued attending the two Baptist

1. Diary [2], 1 Jan. 1758.

2. Diary [2], 1 Jan. 1758.

3. Diary [2], 3 Feb. 1758.

churches, but periodically went to the Methodist Meeting House. For example, on Sunday February 19, he went to the Methodist Meeting in the morning, Oulton's Baptist meeting in the forenoon, and again to the Methodist Meeting in the evening.[4] A month later, he attended an early morning service at the Methodist Meeting and where he records 'heard a good discourse ... from Hosea 6:13.'[5] As stated earlier, Newton also stayed connected to the Established Church, especially to receive the sacrament. For example, in the forenoon of that same day, he took sacrament at St. George's and heard Mr. Maddock[6] preach. 'Though there was something wanting,' Newton recorded, 'I have not heard a better discourse from that quarter [the Established Church] a good while.' In the afternoon, he was back at Mr. Oulton's. That evening he led in family worship and read from Bishop Leighton. He also kept in contact with Whitefield. Newton's diary indicates he wrote to Whitefield, 21 February 1758 but the contents of that letter are unknown. In May, Newton received a guest at the request of Whitefield. 'Met a gentleman from London, Mr. Jay[7], whom dear Mr. G.W. desired to call on me. Spent 3 hours with him.'[8]

---

4. Diary [2], 19 Feb. 1758.

5. Diary [2], 5 March 1758.

6. From 1752, the Rev. Thomas Maddock served as chaplain of St. George's. James Wallace, A *General and Descriptive History of the Ancient and Present State, of the Town of Liverpool*, (Liverpool, 1795), 139. *Gore's Liverpool Directory* (1766), 75 describes him as the incumbent 1753-1767.

7. Identity unknown. Obviously not to be confused with Rev. William Jay (1769-1853) of Bath who became acquainted with Newton in 1788.

8. Diary [2] 18 May 1758.

Early in June, John and Polly travelled to nearby York-shire County to visit where he had heard some churches were experiencing revival and the gospel was flourishing. Upon reaching Leeds, he was delighted to see such vibrant clergy and people. At the end of his stay, he concluded 'what a friendly reception we met with; what a people we found ourselves among ... I hope I shall never forget it. Yet I cannot but say, Happy Leeds! Blessed indeed are the people that are in such a case.'[9] While there, they met John Edwards, a Dissenting minister of White Chapel who for a time had been one of Wesley's itinerants.[10] He heard Edwards preach three times. Next he met Henry Crooke (1708-1770), the evangelical vicar of Hunslet[11] and heard him preach twice, with much pleasure and edification. It was truly a meaningful visit. 'I had many sweet hours and it was with much reluctance I forced myself away on Monday. Our short acquaintance was watered with tears.'[12] In fact, the bond between them had become so close that some of his new friends accompanied Polly and John ten miles out of town. On the way back, they stopped at Haworth where they met and lodged with William Grimshaw (1708-1763),[13] who gave them 'a truly

---

9. Diary [2] 23 June 1758.

10. Ward and Heitzenrater, *Works of John Wesley*, 20:487n.

11. For Crooke (also spelled Crook) see Arthur Pollard, 'Crook, Henry (1708-1770)', *DEB*. 271, 272. Hunslet is now an inner-city area in south Leeds.

12. Diary [2], 23 June 1758.

13. For recent biographies of Grimshaw see the brief, but informative, account by Frank Baker, 'Grimshaw, William', *DEB*, 48; the well-researched volume by Faith Cook, *William Grimshaw of Haworth* (Edinburgh, 1997); and the illustrated guide by Fred Perry, *Travel with William Grimshaw* (Leominster, 2004).

Christian welcome.' He was the colourful and energetic evangelical vicar in Haworth who had an extensive impact in north England. His ministry was marked by numerous revivals and, although he 'sympathised with most moderate elements of Calvinist theology,'[14] was Wesley's designated successor.[15] At the end of that visit, Newton concluded rapturously that 'had it been the will of the Lord methought I could have renounced the world, to have lived in those mountains with a minister and such a people.'[16] Oh how he wished that Liverpool could be like that. Many years later, Newton wrote a brief appreciative biography of Grimshaw, to 'illustrate his extraordinary character.'[17]

When they arrived safely back in Liverpool, Newton reflected on their journey. 'My heart was at times much affected with what I saw and heard and my mouth in some measure opened to give my friends cause to praise the Lord on my behalf.'[18] He was encouraged because not only had he been able to share his case with Edwards, Crooke and Grimshaw, they had encouraged him to pursue his heart's direction. Consequently, he again asked God to lead him in the direction that was 'most fitting.'

---

14. Frank Baker, 'Grimshaw, William', *DEB*, 48.

15. In the end this did not happen because he died in 1763, long before Wesley.

16. Diary [2], 23 June 1758.

17. John Newton, *Memoirs of the life of the late Rev. William Grimshaw ... In six letters to the Rev. Henry Foster* (London, 1799), 1. Because Newton gave the rights and profits of the book to the Society for the Relief of the Poor Clergy, it is not included in the six volume Newton *Works* (Bull, *Newton*, 340).

18. Diary [2], 23 June 1758.

He hoped this would be pastoral ministry, but he submitted to whatever God desired. 'I desire to be anything; to be nothing at thy word.'[19]

This time, he was intent on determining once and for all if he was called of God to pastoral ministry. Therefore, he dedicated the next six weeks to meditate on key Biblical texts related to a call to ministry. He scheduled this enquiry to conclude on his thirty-third birthday. For this special and holy task, he started a separate notebook to record his meditations. He appropriately entitled it *Miscellaneous Thoughts and Enquiries upon an Important Subject.*[20] In it he mentions that others had encouraged him to consider pastoral ministry. He admitted the suggestion made little impression on him at first, but it soon began to take a firmer hold of his mind and heart. He gradually came to 'a readiness to enter that service'[21] but he was still uncertain and desperately wanted to resolve this matter. This was a serious exercise and he proceeded with care and such thoroughness that his notes turned out to be sixty pages in length and about fifteen thousand words. As he came to the end on his birthday, after much soul searching, study, fasting and prayer he solemnly declared his conclusion. 'The day is now arrived when I proposed to close all my deliberations on this subject, with a solemn unreserved, unconditional surrender of my whole self to the Lord. I am now entering upon a new year of life, I now (having met

---

19. Diary [2], 23 June 1758.

20. The MS journal is in the Lambeth Palace, London, item MS 2937. This has now been transcribed by Marylynn Rouse and published by The John Newton Project, Stratford-upon-Avon as *Ministry on My Mind* (2008).

21. 23 June 1758. Rouse, *Ministry on My Mind*, 1.

with nothing to deter me in the time I have taken to consider it) enter upon and give myself up to a new view of life.
From this day I only wait for light and direction when and
where to move and to begin; and for this I pray to wait pa-
tiently till I clearly see the Lord going before me and making me a plain plan.'[22] He concluded with five resolutions
to guide his path forward and stated his resolve. 'When
I go from hence I shall take my refreshment with a thankful heart humbly trusting that the Lord has accepted my
desire and that in his good time he will both appoint me
work, and furnish me with grace, wisdom and strength to
perform it.'[23] Returning now to his regular diary he wrote,
'I have nothing now to do but to wait and to pray till the
Lord shall in his Providence to make a way plain for me to
set out.' Using language of Luke 9:62, he vowed, 'having
put my hand to the plough, I will not look back.'[24] As he
said later to Clunie, 'As to laying aside all thoughts of the
ministry, it is quite out of my power; I cannot, I will not
give up the desire; though I shall not run before I am sent.
I agree with you that my call has not yet been made clear,
because I think no one's call is compleat* till the Lord has
confirmed their desire by his providence, and placed them
in the work.'[25] Newton firmly believed he had the inward
call and now he waited for the outward call.

Applications to the Established Church
Though, on one hand, Newton said he had nothing to do
but wait, this did not mean that he was idle. He set up

22. 4 Aug. 1758. Rouse, *Ministry on My Mind*, 20.

23. 4 Aug. 1758. Rouse, *Ministry on my Mind*, 24.

24. Diary [2] 4 Aug. 1758.

25. Newton to Clunie, 30 July 1762, Newton (Clunie), 13.

a religious society of men that met every Thursday evening at Oulton's chapel and he served as the moderator. After the third meeting, Newton noticed that he had been 'favoured with light and liberty' beyond what he expected.[26] This he interpreted as a further confirmation that he was fitted for ministry. He also corresponded with Crooke in Leeds who had encouraged him to pursue ministry in the Established Church. That appealed to Newton who explained his hesitation about other denominations. 'I love and honour all that love the Lord Jesus, but the Congregational plan was too narrow for either my judgment or inclination, and many difficulties stood in the way of joining Methodists though I rejoice in their usefulness, and regard them as a people whom the Lord had called and owned.'[27] He does not give specific details. Nor does he mention the Baptists because, although he regularly attended the local Baptist churches, he disagreed with them over believers' baptism.

Trying to sort out his options, Newton confessed he was burdened for the residents of Liverpool. 'It is with great concern ... that I see forty thousand people here the far greatest part of whom I fear are strangers to the way of salvation.' He continues, 'The first choice of my heart (if it dared to choose for itself) would be, for an opportunity to preach the Gospel in this place.'[28] Since this option was unlikely, his second choice was to serve in Yorkshire

---

26. Diary [2] 4 Aug. 1758.

27. Newton to Rev. Henry Crooke, of Leeds, 9 Nov. 1758. MSS in West Yorkshire Archive Service, Catalogue Ref CL. Transcriptions courtesy of Marylynn Rouse.

28. Newton to Crooke, Nov 20, 1758.

and be with or near Crooke, and then annually return to preach in Liverpool, if pulpits would be open to him.

On Saturday 18 November 1758, he received two letters from Crooke offering Newton to be his curate and 'promising a title,' though the details still had to be worked out. Further, Crooke pressed him immediately to seek ordination. Newton responded positively to Crooke's gracious offer. He finished a draft of five sermons he had been working on, with one more to go. When on 9 December he received the good news from Crooke that everything was ready for him to be Crook's curate, he went to request the three required testimonials from clergy. The first three he approached gave him a mixed response. The first said no. The second 'promised in general' and the third 'wished him success', but they all were afraid to support a 'suspected Methodist.' Not one to give up, Newton continued making his rounds to these and other clergy, including the Dean who gave him 'a friendly reception.' [29]

As soon as he finally was able to obtain the three testimonials, on the way he picked up the signed documents from Crooke and anxiously continued on to London to meet the Bishop of Chester in the House of Lords. The Bishop greeted him 'with great civility' but explained that, though Liverpool at the time was in Chester diocese, Newton's intended church was in the Archdiocese of York. So he went to his office but was unable to meet him in person. But he did get an answer. Newton quickly relayed the sad outcome to Polly. 'Well! All is over.' He goes on to explain: 'He [the Bishop of Chester]

29. Diary [2], 9, 10 Dec. 1758.

countersigned my testimonials and directed me to Dr. Newton, the archbishop's chaplain. On him I waited this morning. He referred me to the secretary, and from him I received the softest refusal imaginable. He had represented my affair to the archbishop, but his Grace was inflexible in supporting the *rules and canons* of the church.'[30] Newton described it as 'the softest refusal possible.' However, Aitken is probably more accurate when he says it was 'in reality a harsh rejection, equivalent to a slap in the face.'[31] The 'rules and canons' refer to Canon 34 that state that ordination candidates are to be graduates of either Cambridge or Oxford. Though this was the official policy, many clergy did not have such a degree. This is why Crooke offered Newton the curacy and had encouraged Newton to proceed in the first place. But on this occasion, the Archbishop of this diocese was inflexible.

Newton, no doubt trying not to worry Polly, reassured her that he was feeling 'quite satisfied and easy' because God 'could open another door in a minute.' However, a week later, reality hit Newton who now confessed to Polly that he could 'neither write, nor pray, nor talk to purpose' and that he was 'quiet, dry, and barren.'[32] This was understandable because the shock of denial was so swift and final. So while he was in London, and probably to debrief, he met with William Romaine. And on the way home he met with Dr. Young , the rector in Welwyn who received him very courteously and encouraged him

---

30. *Letters to a Wife*, 20 Dec. 1758 in *Works* 5:521.

31. Aitken, Newton, 153.

32. Newton to Polly, 28 Dec. 1758, quoted in Aitken, *Newton*, 155. Original at Lambeth Palace, MS 2935 (f. 24).

in his desire to enter the ministry.[33] But the future was uncertain, so he returned to his job as Tide Surveyor and prayed for a new spirit for the task.

With Crooke's encouragement, he applied a second time. This time, however, he gathered his necessary papers and sent them directly to the Archbishop of York. The previous application had been somewhat rushed because the Bishop of Chester had passed him on to the Archbishop, without notice. Therefore Newton hoped that this time, by giving the Archbishop more time to review the material and check out references, etc., the response would be positive. But within two weeks he received a flat refusal with no explanation from Richard Chapman, the Archbishop's secretary. 'I herewith return you my Lord Archbishop of York's order ... that his Grace, having been informed that you have an employment in the Custom House at Liverpool, in which you have been for some time, his Grace thinks it is best for you to continue in that station that Providence had placed you in, and that his Grace, therefore desires to be excused admitting you into Holy Orders.'[34]

Newton noted the 'flat refusal' in his diary, and lifted up his voice in prayer. 'O Lord, thou art my hope and the object of my views and vows, do thou order all my concerns according to thy wisdom and goodness.' He continued, 'When thou wilt, where and how thou wilt, only comfort me with thy presence and enable me to wait on

---

33. Cecil/Rouse, *Newton*, 87, 342.

34. Richard Chapman to John Newton, Feb. 10, 1758. Quoted in Aitken, *Newton*, 376, endnote.

thee alone.'[35] The news of Newton's rejection apparently spread in town, for a few days later he recorded 'the refusal of my ordination makes much noise.'[36] Nevertheless, that same day (21 Feb. 1759) he resolved not to give up. 'I have not yet determined how to proceed; it seems incumbent on me to require farther* explanation [from the Archbishop] .... Perhaps it may not be the will of God that I should appear on that side [the Established Church]; but I think to pursue my application during this year.'[37]

Consequently two months later, he tried a third time. This time he applied to the Bishop of Chester (who was Bishop over Liverpool). He recorded this effort in his diary, 5 April 1759. 'I wrote to the Bishop of Chester renewing the suit in which I was lately repulsed. I think it incumbent on me to pursue the means and I hope I am quite willing to leave the event with the Lord.' Two weeks later, he received the much-awaited response to his application; but it was not what he wanted. The answer on behalf of the Bishop was quite official and final: 'Whatever sentiments the Bishop might have on your case, yet the Archbishop's refusal of you has *absolutely tied up his hands* from attending any further application [emphasis added].'[38]

Newton's three efforts to be ordained covered a span of about six exhausting months (Dec. 1758-May 1759).

---

35. Diary [2], 13 Feb. 1759.

36. Diary [2], 21 Feb. 1759.

37. Diary [2], 21 Feb. 1759.

38. This letter, 17 May 1759, is cited in *Historical Manuscripts Commission. XV report, Appendix, Part 1, The Manuscripts of the Earl of Dartmouth*, vol. III (London, 1896), 173.

Further, during the third effort, Newton learned that on his own Crooke had asked Henry Venn[39] (who through Lord Dartmouth's patronage had recently become vicar in Huddersfield, West Yorkshire) to ask Dartmouth to advocate for Newton.[40] So when Newton received his third denial, he quickly bundled his documents of the proceedings and sent them to Dartmouth. In Newton's cover letter, he indicated what first launched his desire to be a pastor. 'My first and principal motive was that I might, if possible, repair some of the evil effects of my former life.'[41] Later that month, Newton heard back from Lord Dartmouth. Though it was 'a very obliging spiritual letter,' once again Newton received a negative response. 'He sees but little reason to expect my admission into the vineyard by the Episcopal door.'[42] Newton also heard from Romaine. 'About the same time, [I] received one from Mr. Romaine putting me in mind of the shortness of life and advising me, if quite shut on that side [i.e., the Established Church], to apply and begin elsewhere as fast as possible.'[43]

The next year Newton shared his sad story with John Wesley who was appalled. 'I had a good deal of

---

39. Venn (1725-1797) before being appointed vicar in Huddersfield, Yorkshire in 1759, had served as curate in Clapham, near London (1754-1759). His son John became vicar in Clapham in 1796 where he was influential in the Clapham Sect and friend of Wilberforce (Clyde Ervine, 'Venn, Henry (1724-1797)', *DEB*, 1137-1138).

40. Diary [2] 21 May 1759.

41. Newton to Dartmouth, 22 May 1759, *Historical Manuscripts Commission ... Dartmouth*, 172.

42. Diary [2] 22 June 1759.

43. Diary [2] 22 June 1759.

conversation with Mr. N[ewto]n. His case is very peculiar. Our Church requires that clergymen should be men of learning and to this end have an university education. But how many have an* university education and yet no learning at all! Yet these men are ordained! Meantime one of eminent learning, as well as unblameable* behaviour, cannot be ordained, "because he was not at the university"! What a mere farce is this! Who would believe that any Christian bishop would stoop to so poor an evasion!'[44]

During his seeking-ordination process, just to be safe, Newton was careful not to be associated openly with Methodists, because of the prejudice of many (especially the hierarchy) in the Established Church. For example when Wesley came to Liverpool in May 1759, he chose to go to only one public meeting, though he met with him privately. [45] So now that the door to the Established Church was closed, Newton resumed his normal public habits. He mentions the following on his trip to London. 'I heard Mr. Whitefield tonight for the first time, for I have cautiously avoided all intercourse with those deem'd Methodists that I might not throw hindrances in my own way.'[46] He also published the six discourses that he had originally prepared to help him in the ordination process and hopefully preach in his first church. The title was *Six Discourses (or Sermons), as Intended for the Pulpit* (1760) [47] and in the preface he explained his reasons.

---

44. Wesley diary, 20 March 1760, in Ward and Heitzenrater, *Works of John Wesley*, 21: 248.

45. Diary [2], 4 May 1759.

46. Quoted in Martin, *Newton*, 185.

47. *Works* 2:256-354.

'The following discourses were drawn up about twelve months since, when I expected a speedy opportunity of delivering them from the pulpit. As the views I had then are now over-ruled, I take this method of laying them before the public.'[48] He sent out copies to acquaintances, including one copy to Lord Dartmouth, who received it with thanks and after reading it, spoke well of it.[49]

A Temporary Call

In December 1759, Newton received an unexpected invitation to consider becoming pastor of an Independent congregation in Warwick, near Stratford-upon-Avon and approximately 130 miles south of Liverpool. This young congregation, Cow Lane Chapel, was constructing their new building and in need of a pastor.[50] Brewer had strongly recommended Newton to them.[51] Therefore, the congregation invited him to 'make trial' of his gifts and 'if it should be the will of God to undertake the charge' of the church.[52] He recorded his thoughts in his diary. 'Though I am constantly praying for a call and opportunity to set out, I tremble whenever there seems to be a prospect opening.' So he prayed, 'Oh Lord God, I am a child and cannot speak. They [the congregation] are as yet but a few people, but it is a large town, and in a situation that might afford

---

48. *Works* 2: 257.

49. Diary [2], 9 Feb.1760; 7 April 1760.

50. Diary [2], 23 Dec. 1759; Bull, *Newton*, 104. Cecil/Rouse, *Newton*, 98, indicates that Cow Lane was later renamed Brook Street and the church building is presently used for commercial offices.

51. 'Memoir of the Late Rev. J. Newton,' *The Evangelical Magazine* (1808), 98.

52. Diary [2], 23 Dec. 1759.

a prospect of usefulness, if the Lord should vouchsafe his blessing. With him I leave it.'[53] The next week he wrote to Brewer and Romaine in London about the Warwick situation.[54] The week following he wrote to Whitefield, but his diary only states 'wrote to G.W.'.[55] But no doubt it was about Warwick too. Romaine responded by urging Newton accept the invitation and accept the call, if given.[56] He also met with Oulton and wrote to John Wesley.[57] Newton decided to accept the invitation and received permission for three-months leave of absence, when needed. Wisely, he used the intervening months before going in April, 'devoted to spiritual things' and preparing sermons.[58] Though it would be only a three-month term as a lay pastor, he wanted to be prepared.

When the time came (it turned out to be May, not April as planned), he first took Polly to Chatham so she could stay with her family. On his way to Warwick he stopped in London and informed Polly of this stopover. 'Next morning scratch'd up pretty early to hear Mr. Whitefield. After [the] sermon breakfasted with him. I wish you were with me ... I am sure he would please you... . Mr. W[hitefiel]d seem'd greatly pleas'd to find I was desirous to engage in the good work some way or other.'[59] To

---

53. Diary [2], 23 Dec. 1759.

54. Diary [2], 24, 25 Dec. 1759.

55. Diary [2], 31 Dec. 1759.

56. Diary [2], 1 Jan. 1760.

57. Diary [2], 2, 4 Jan. 1760. The content of the letter to Wesley is not known, but probably it was concerning Warwick.

58. Diary [2], 4 March 1760.

59. From portion of letter quoted Martin, *Newton*, 191.

Whitefield, who was not one to be idle in ministry, it was important to keep going forward. So when ministry through one door (The Established Church) was closed, it made sense to go through this open door to Warwick even though it was short-term and in a small independent congregation. He further encouraged Newton by saying, 'those who could speak a word for the promoting the cause of religion ought by no means to be silent.'[60]

At the end of the trial period (May, June, July), the congregation responded positively and desired him to be their pastor. This was a crucial decision so he returned to Liverpool to pray further about it and seek counsel of pastoral friends. He ventured over to Yorkshire where he stayed three days with Grimshaw in Haworth, visited with friends in the Leeds area, and lodged overnight with Venn at Huddersfield. By mid-October, through the counsel of friends (he specifically mentions Brewer's counsel) he decided not to accept the call. Soon after he informed the congregation, two members from the Warwick congregation arrived and prevailed upon him 'to break through [his] difficulties and settle among them.'[61] When they said 'the desire of the people is so earnest and unanimous,' Newton thought he could not resist because, as he thought, 'I cannot but think it amounts to a clear call.' However, he was still uncertain so he asked the Warwick congregation to join him in praying for further direction.

In the end, Newton declined the call. It is unclear what the issues were. When he received the first call, Newton

---

60. From transcription of the MS letter above by Marylynn Rouse.
61. Diary [2], 1 Nov. 1760.

already noted that one difficulty was with 'respects to the settlement' arrangements.[62] Further communication revealed that the congregation was not as harmonious as he was first led to believe. This was seen in the mixed messages he was now receiving from congregational members, especially from one of their leaders, Mr.Vennor.[63] In addition, some of his pastoral friends encouraged him not to accept. Brewer, who knew the congregation and at first had been keen on it, advised against it, possibly because he was aware of internal issues. Also Anglican clergy (Henry Crooke of Hunslet and Henry Venn of Huddersfield) cautioned him not to give up on the Established Church.[64] In addition to this, Aitken points out that Polly and her family were not in favour of him joining the Dissenters.[65] In all probability, it was a combination of all these factors. In contrast, Whitefield may have been the one voice encouraging him to accept the call to Warwick. Newton's diary entry probably has a reference to Whitefield with whom he was corresponding at the time and who had earlier expressed something similar to Newton on the way to Warwick. 'Rec'd a letter from Mr. W. very kind as usual but he differs *toto coelo* [Lat. diametrically] from Mr. B. he [Mr. W.] would have me by all means push to the utmost in aiming at usefulness, without regard to expectations or consequences, but leave all the rest in the hand of God.'[66]

---

62. Diary [2], 1 Aug. 1760. For discussion of possible reasons, see Hindmarsh, *Newton*, 93, 94.

63. Bull, *Newton*, 111.

64. Aitken, *Newton*, 161.

65. Aitken, *Newton*, 161. See also Martin, *Newton*, 192, 193.

66. Diary [2], 3 Mar. 1761. He had written to Mr. W., 25 Feb. 1761.

Twenty some years later, Newton shared his perspective with Richard Cecil (1745-1810), one of the many young pastors who regularly met with him in London for conversation and prayer. Newton's dry wit mixed with wisdom shines in his comment on his Warwick experience. 'I remember, in going to undertake the care of a congregation (in Warwick) I was reading as I walked in a green lane: "Fear not, Paul, I have much people in this city" [Act 18:10]. But I soon afterwards was disappointed in finding that Paul was not John and that Corinth was not Warwick.'[67]

An Unexpected Call

As stated earlier, Newton's original desire was to serve as pastor within the Established Church. But because of the three firm rejections, he basically had given up on this aspiration. Two years after the Warwick affair, he expressed it this way to Rev. Caleb Warhurst, a pastor of an Independent chapel in Manchester. 'I have quite done with the Established Church, so called – not out of anger or despair, but from the conviction that the Lord has been wise & good in disappointing my views in that quarter.' In fact, he so resigned himself to the closed door in that direction, that he went on to say, 'And I believe if the admission I once so earnestly sought was now freely offered me, I could hardly, if at all, accept it.'[68]

Providentially, at about the same time in late 1762, Newton received two innocent requests that were

---

67. Richard Cecil included this comment in his list of remarks that Newton had made (Cecil/Rouse, *Newton*, 215).

68. Newton to Caleb Warhurst, [in late September 1762], Timothy D. Whelan, ed., *Baptist Autographs in the John Rylands University Library of Manchester, 1741-1845* (Macon, Ga., 2009), 9.

instrumental in him becoming well-known and in eventually opening the closed door to the Established Church. The first request was from John Fawcett (1740-1817), the pastor of Wainsgate Baptist Church near Hebden Bridge, West Yorkshire. He had been converted through a sermon by George Whitefield and for a time was a Methodist until, at age twenty-four, he switched and became pastor of the Baptist church. He remained near the place of his birth in West Yorkshire for his full ministry, though twice he was invited to leave the small town and move south to major places of ministry. He turned them both down.[69] He is known today as the hymn writer who wrote *Blest be the Tie that Binds* and *Lord Dismiss Us with Thy Blessing*. Fawcett asked him to write up his life story. Newton agreed and in October sent it in the form of eight letters.[70]

The second request came from Thomas Haweis (1734-1820) who at that time was a curate to Martin Madan at Lock Hospital in London. He saw the eight letters that Fawcett had received and was much moved by them. But he wanted more details so he asked Newton to write an expanded version. Newton complied by sending it in instalments, in the form of letters. In the process, he wanted to end his biography with his marriage to Polly, but Haweis wanted him to continue. Consequently, Newton provided further details, including his additional journeys

---

69. In 1772, he was called to follow John Gill at Carter Lane Baptist church, London, that is now known as Metropolitan (Spurgeon's) Tabernacle and in 1792 was invited to the presidency of Bristol Baptist Academy, Bristol (E. F. Clipson, 'Fawcett, John', *DEB*, 381).

70. Diary [2], 28 Oct. 1762.

on the seas, his spiritual growth, and his meeting Clunie, Brewer and Whitefield.[71] At the end of his final letter, number fourteen, he shared about his burden to be a pastor and the frustrated application to the Archbishop. He wisely described this discreetly and did not mention that he had been rejected three times. He ended by expressing his submission to the will of God. 'At present I desist my applications. My desire to serve the Lord is not weakened; but I am not so hasty to push myself forward as I was formerly. It is sufficient that he knows how to dispose of me, and that he both can and will do what is best.'[72]

The decision was made to publish these letters, but for some unknown reason his autobiography, *An Authentic Narrative of Some Remarkable and Interesting Particulars in the Life of* ******* *Communicated in a Series of Letters to the Reverend Mr. Haweis* [73] was not published until eighteen months after it was completed. But when it was published in August 1764, it quickly became quite popular and is still being published today, under various titles.[74] However prior

---

71. Aitken, *Newton*, 165-170.

72. Letter 14, *An Authentic Narrative*, 94.

73. The full title shows that when it was first published, Newton's identity was hidden and Haweis had moved to Aldwincle. *An Authentic Narrative of Some Remarkable and Interesting Particulars in the Life of* ***** *Communicated in a Series of Letters to the Rev. Mr. Haweis, Rector of Aldwincle, Northamptonshire and by Him (at the request of Friends) Now Made Public* (London, 1764).

74. For example, *John Newton, Out of the Depths* (Moody Press, n.d.); *Life and Spirituality of John Newton*, intro by Bruce Hindmarsh (Regent College, 2003) which also includes three letters on spiritual growth; and *Slaver Captain: John Newton*, ed. by Vincent McInerney (Seaforth, 2010) which includes *Thoughts on the African Slave Trade* (1788). McInerney's book is slightly abridged and modernised for present readership.

to this, Haweis was circulating the unpublished draft to friends, including Lord Dartmouth.

That same year a pastoral position (as curate) became available in Olney and Dartmouth, who owned the living for the Established Church of St. Peter and St. Paul in the town offered it to Haweis. But just prior to this, Newton had asked Haweis for advice because he was being pursued by a Presbyterian church near Halifax, West Yorkshire. Therefore, knowing this, Haweis recommended Newton for the position in Olney.[75] Dartmouth, as stated earlier had corresponded with Newton in the past and read the unpublished draft of his autobiography. Previously, when Newton approached Dartmouth for help in 1759, Dartmouth indicated that he did not think anything could be done to overcome the Archbishop's refusals. But this time, being impressed with Newton's unwavering desire to be a pastor, having Haweis' strong endorsement, and now with one of his own livings available, Dartmouth agreed to pursue the matter. Consequently, on 4 March 1764, Newton received Dartmouth's official offer of the living at Olney. In addition, Dartmouth wrote directly to the Bishop of Chester, who had twice turned down Newton and who now with Dartmouth's positive report, agreed to countersign the testimonials. To help pave the way further for Newton, Lord Dartmouth visited the Bishop of Lincoln, in whose diocese Olney was located. Despite this, when Newton arrived, the Bishop sent him to the new Archbishop of York who was holding ordination services. On arrival, Richard Chapman (who was the secretary for the previous archbishop who had

---

75. A. Skevington Wood, *Thomas Haweis* (London, 1957), 100, 101.

turned down Newton) responded, 'Sir, not to mince the matter, you know you were formerly disappointed. His Grace has heard of it and desires to be excused.'[76]Newton shared the disappointing news with Dartmouth who quickly drafted a direct appeal to the Archbishop, which Newton immediately took back to him. Despite this, the archbishop opted out of doing it personally (probably because his predecessor had denied Newton). Instead he sent a personal note back to Dartmouth promising that the Bishop of Lincoln would ordain Newton. When informed of this, the Bishop of Lincoln agreed, interviewed Newton and on 29 April 1764 ordained him a deacon and formally made him an Anglican priest, 17 June 1764.[77] Aitken honours the key role Dartmouth played in Newton's ordination by declaring he was instrumental in 'converting the reluctant bishops from washing their hands of Newton into laying their hands upon him.'[78] For five and a half years it had been a hot potato that those in the Church hierarchy were afraid to touch.

The day before he was to be ordained a deacon, he shared the wonderful news with Polly. 'I now almost stagger at the prospect before me ... I am to stand in a very public point of view, to take charge of a large parish, ... to preach what I ought and to be what I preach.' Aware of the momentous responsibilities before him, Newton knew he could not proceed without God's help. 'Oh!

---

76. Aitken, *Newton*, 175.

77. Details are from Aitken, *Newton*, 171-177 and Hindmarsh, *Newton*, 103-106.

78. Aitken, *Newton*, 177.

what zeal, faith, patience, watchfulness, and courage will be needful for my support and guidance! My only hope is in the name and power of Jesus.' He was aware that his change in vocation placed demands on Polly too, so he includes her in his closing prayer. 'May that precious name be as ointment poured forth to *your* soul and mine! May that power be triumphantly manifested in *our* weakness [emphasis added]!' On his way home, he understandably stopped in at Olney 'to peep at the place and people.'[79]

On returning to Liverpool, he and Polly began packing. When he went back to thank the clergy who had written their testimonials in his ordination application, they asked him to preach before he moved to Olney. This was a daunting challenge for him. 'I found the thoughts of preaching, where I was so generally known, was alarming to me, yet I durst not (nor indeed I could not desire to) decline it.' He had long prayed for an opportunity to minister in his town. At last, he had the opportunity. 'I knew many or most would be willing to hear me, and I hoped the Lord might make my word useful to some.'[80] To start 'gradually,' he preached first to a small Sunday congregation in nearby Crosby.[81] He felt he preached with liberty and was 'tolerably well received.' That was without notes, so he thought he would do the same the following Thursday at St. George's where he had often

---

79. *Letters to a Wife*, 28 April 1764, in *Works* 5:541.

80. Unless indicated otherwise, all the details and quotes in the paragraph are from Newton's Diary [2].

81. Newton fondly remembered that his first sermon was at Crosby, near Liverpool on the first Sunday of May 1764 as stated ten years later in his Diary [3], 1 May 1774.

attended.[82] But this time, the large and varied congregation had a mixed response. 'Some were pleased but many were *disgusted*.' In the eighteenth-century this word meant *displeased* and is less harsh.[83] They complained that he preached 'too long, too loud, [and] too much extempore.' He admitted, 'I did speak a little too loud at Liverpool the first time, because I knew not the extent of my voice, nor how much was necessary in a large congregation; but I corrected it afterwards.' [84] Learning from this experience, Newton preached shorter sermons and with notes the following Sunday at the 'old church' (St. Nicholas) in the morning and St. Peter's (for the infirmary) in the afternoon. The next two Sundays he preached at nearby Childwell to a congregation which included friends and others from Liverpool. Despite preaching six sermons, each from a different text, he was satisfied and believed that God had blessed his efforts. 'He enabled me to preach the truth before many thousands,' he reported to Clunie and 'I hope with some measure of success, and in general with much greater acceptance than I could have expected.'[85]

Newton's anguishing process of seeking to become a pastor finally came to an end. As a seaman, he had been

---

82. Martin , *Newton*, 202 states that in the congregation that day sat his co-workers, town dignitaries and his long-time employer, Joseph Manesty sitting in the Town Clerk's pew. For the occasion, Newton wore the gown and cassock that Martin Madan, the noted London preacher at the Lock, gave him 'as a token of love.' All this may have been true, but Martin provides no footnotes to verify this.

83. Aitken, *Newton*, 180.

84. Newton to Clunie, 21 June 1764, Newton (Clunie), 32.

85. Newton to Clunie, 1 June 1764, Newton (Clunie), 25.

based in Liverpool for almost seven years and as a Tide Surveyor, he had lived there for eight. Now this Liverpool chapter of his life was completed and he and Polly said goodbye to their friends and set out for Olney. He recorded these details in his diary and then did something unusual, but quite symbolic in his diary. He left the remaining one-third of the page blank and turned the page to begin recording the new chapter in his life. Yet, he did not forget his friends and his church connections there or his burden for Liverpool. For example, three years later in 1767 he returned for a week where he preached once in St. Peter's, twice in the 'old church' and once in St. George's.[86]

---

86. Diary [1767], 16-23 April.

Photo Gallery

Whitefield preaching in Moorfields, 1742

Left: mostly rowdy hecklers, including a clown on shoulders with whip and trumpeter in tree.

Centre: woman on steps collecting response notes; mother below praying, possibly over her sick child.

Right: attentive listeners; drummer sent to disrupt by marching through.

This event, described on pages 159, 160, is portrayed in the painting 'Whitefield preaching at Moorfields, 1742' by Eyre Crowe (1824-1910) in 1865. The engraving of it, shown here, appeared in the *Illustrated London News* 22 July 1865. This edition of the paper is in the possession of the author.

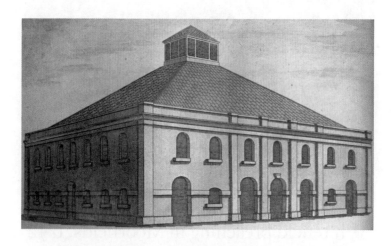

Whitefield's Tabernacle, Moorfields

Drawn by John Groves, 1772

Image courtesy of the Evangelical Library, London.

This was built in 1753 to replace the twelve-year-old wooden Tabernacle. Two years later, it was here that John Newton first heard Whitefield. The brick building was eighty feet square and with a gallery on each of its four sides it was capable of cramming in four thousand people. Not shown next-door was the Tabernacle House that served as a residence for George and Elizabeth Whitefield and a headquarters for the ministry (Dallimore, *Whitefield* 2:355-357).

George Whitefield statue

This full statue of Whitefield is the only one in the world and is located at the University of Pennsylvania, in Philadelphia, Pennsylvania. See further details, page 135.

Photo courtesy of the Evangelical Library, London.

came to speak to ye case of Gods withdrawing his gracious presence 248
from a believer, & departing from him for a season, for a total & final
departure he said (& blessed be God he said as it is written) we are freed
from by the covenant of grace & the assurance of his everlasting love.
He shewd first ye usual causes as spiritual pride, careless sinful
walk, love of ye world, vain conversation, waste of time & talents &c.
2ly the marks of it, barreness & deadness with regard to duties &
ordinances, a remiss conduct making light of small sins as they are
by some called, & at length a callous insensible disposition, which
makes us think all peace & well, while we are upon the brink of
ruin. this in kind harderd upon total apostacy, & would infalibly
end in it could we be left to ourselves, but in such a state God will
in mercy find us out, & either by outward forrovidences or spiritual humblings, will bring us to seek him again, &
feel & acknowledge it to be an evil & a bitter thing that ever we
provoked him to forsake us. The application was 1st to those who
have present communion & trusted thro rich mercy that was
then in measure my case, he exorted such to be very careful of
avoiding all the mentioned causes of Gods departure, & whatever
we experimentally found tending to weaken & lessen our spiritual
frame, & to be much in secret prayer. 2ly those who have had communion & have now lost it, he directed to renew their applications to the
Ld. J. C. for restitution of his spirit & concluded 3ly with an awful
caution to sinners, who never had Gods presence nor ever were troubled
about the want of it, but what he said on this subject was so peculiar to himself that I cannot attempt it. The whole of his discourse
was extraordinary & expressive. Spent the evening at Mr. Thorpes

John Newton's diary

This is 2/3 of a page (see Sermon 6, pp. 57-59) in Newton's diary
(C0 199) in the Department of Rare Books and Special Collections,
Princeton University.

Image courtesy of Princeton University Library.

Church of St. Peter and St. Paul, Olney

As seen here today, the tall spire of the church stands high above the town of Olney. Newton served here 1764-1780.

Photo courtesy of Michael Brace (www.geograph.org.uk).

Newton's vicarage in Olney

Lord Dartmouth enlarged and renovated the vicarage for Newton whose study was in the attic with his dormer window on the far right. This home now a private residence.

Photo courtesy of Robert Drayton (www.geograph.org.uk).

Verses on wall in Newton's study

These are the actual verses that Newton had painted on the wall above the fireplace in his study. As he explained to Lord Dartmouth, this was to keep "reminding me from day to day what I was [in Africa], and by what means I am now undeservedly settled in the Vicarage at Olney" (*Historical Manuscripts Commission... Earl of Dartmouth*, 186).

Photo courtesy of John Crotts.

St. Mary Woolnoth, London

Newton served here from 1780 till his death, 21 Dec. 1807. This drawing, that was done a few years after Newton's time, shows the church on the left and busy King William Street on the right.

Drawing in the possession of the author.

5

Ministry in Olney (1764-1779)

A Town Prepared By Whitefield

Olney was a small, somewhat isolated market village, about sixty miles northwest of London. The parish included about 500 houses and 2,000 inhabitants.[1] When Newton began his ministry there, he was thirty-nine and Polly, his wife of fourteen years, was thirty-five. He was appointed curate-in-charge and Moses Browne (the vicar who was leaving Olney) remained the official vicar of the church, though he had accepted the chaplaincy at Morden College, ninety miles away.[2] Newton's salary was much less than what he received in Liverpool.[3] But that did not matter because his heart's desire was to serve as a pastor. His ministry was well received and the congregation grew so much they had to increase the seating. In addition, Lord Dartmouth renovated and enlarged the vicarage for John and Mary so they could provide hospitality to their many guests and travelling preachers. He also renovated a large home (nicknamed *The Great House*)

---

1. Hindmarsh, *Newton*, 170.

2. Aitken, *Newton*, 190.

3. Newton's official income was to be £60 per year, but £20 of this was to be given to Browne. Newton did not mind this because he knew Browne had a large family to support.

that he owned next to the church so Newton could use it for mid-week meetings.

It is significant that when Newton arrived in Olney in 1764, he came to a community that had already been positively influenced by Whitefield. Consequently, Olney was primed to be receptive to Newton's evangelical ministry.[4] It is astonishing that Whitefield had previously visited Olney eight times and preached at least nine times in this small town (in contrast there is no record of Wesley visiting there).[5] The details following are gleaned from Luke Tyerman, *The Life of George Whitefield*, 2 vols. (1877).

a. In May, 1739, at the age of twenty-four Whitefield made his first visit to Olney, but the pastor (Wolsey Johnson) of the Established Church refused to open his pulpit. So Whitefield responded by preaching to about 2000 gathered in a field. Afterwards, he went to Northampton, twelve miles from Olney, where he met with Dr. Phillip Doddridge, the famous pastor-educator, and preached to large crowds. On his way back to Bedford, he stopped in Olney, because they had 'begged' to see him once more. Again, he preached in the open air, this time despite the heavy rain. (Tyerman, 1:231)

Whitefield recorded the event in his journal.

'Great numbers were assembled together; but on account of it being a rainy day, it was judged inconvenient to preach in the fields. I there-

---

4. See Hindmarsh, *Newton*, 169-186 for helpful religious background on Olney.

5. Olney is not mentioned in the index of Ward and Heitzenrater, *Works of John Wesley*, 24:653.

fore stood upon an eminence in the street, and preached from thence with such a power as I have not for some time experienced. Though it rained all the time, yet the people stood very attentive and patient. All, I really believe, *felt*, as well as *heard* the Word, and one was so pricked to the heart, and convinced of sin, that I scarce saw the like instance.[6]

When Newton arrived, he acknowledged the results of this 1739 visit. 'We have several precious souls of so long standing in the kingdom of God. Soon after a little place was built, a society formed and Mr. Whitefield's preachers came frequently.'[7] In October 1744, one of Whitefield's preachers, Thomas Lewis, mentions speaking in the Tabernacle in Olney for a full week resulting in many conversions. And just a few miles north in Northampton he said, 'the people seem to be all in a flame, and stretched after God.' (Tyerman, 2:112)

b. On 4 September 1748 on his way to Scotland, Whitefield wrote from Olney, 'in the church, tabernacle and fields, the congregations have been great.' He does not mention preaching on this visit, but one could not imagine him not ministering in some way. (Tyerman, 2:196)

c. On 6 May 1750 on his way to a northern tour, he preached twice to great crowds in Olney and in the next two days in Northampton, he met with

---

6. George Whitefield's Journal (Edinburgh, 1960) quoted in Hindmarsh, *Newton*, 183.

7. *Twenty-five Letters of John Newton* (Edinburgh, 1840), 66, 67. See also Hindmarsh, *Newton*, 183.

Doddridge and James Hervey and 'preached to above two thousand in a field.' (Tyerman, 2:256)

d. In June 1753, on his way to the north, he 'had two good meetings' at Olney and several thousand attended in Northampton. (Tyerman, 2:310)

e. In October 1753, he visited Olney twice, on the sixth and the eleventh, where he preached each time and reported 'a blessed season at Olney.' (Tyerman, 2:315)

f. In July 1758, on his way to Scotland, he preached in Olney. He also spoke in John Bunyan's pulpit in Bedford, in the field in Northampton and for the recently converted John Berridge,[8] pastor at Everton. He reported 'good seasons at all places.'(Tyerman, 2:410)

A Ministry Supported By Friends Of Whitefield

It was also significant that Newton's patron, Lord Dartmouth, was an ardent supporter of the Evangelical Revival, and especially of Whitefield. For example in 1757, he asked Lady Huntingdon to encourage Whitefield and Romaine to come to his town of Cheltenham. When Whitefield arrived, Lord and Lady Dartmouth accompanied him to the local church. When Whitefield found himself locked out by the resistant rector he climbed atop a large nearby tombstone and spoke in power to the immense crowd gathered to hear him. Henry Venn, one of the evangelical clergy in attendance, enthusiastically reported the events to Lady Huntingdon. 'O with what

8. For an appreciative, yet candid, brief biography see J.C. Ryle, *Five Christian Leaders of the Eighteenth Century* (1868, Edinburgh, reprint 1960), 116-148.

eloquence, energy, and melting tenderness, did Mr. Whitefield beseech sinners to be reconciled to God.'[9] Many were so impacted that Venn and three other clergy (Martin Madan, William Talbot[10] and George Downing[11]) spanned out into the crowd where they sought to 'comfort those broken down under a sense of guilt.'[12] The next morning, Whitefield preached to a large crowd. In the evening, Talbot preached at Lord Dartmouth's residence to as many as the rooms could handle. Afterwards hundreds lingered outside wanting to hear Whitefield again. In response, though exhausted from preaching that morning, he stood upon a table near the front of the mansion and preached once more. Whitefield was not one to turn down an opportunity to preach and Lord and Lady Dartmouth were not ashamed to throw open their doors for Whitefield and his fellow evangelicals.[13] The next day, Charles Wesley and many friends joined them at Dartmouth's and the meetings continued.

While serving in Olney, Newton was also helped by another ardent supporter of Whitefield. He was John Thornton (1720-1790), the brother of Mrs. Hanna

---

9. Venn to Lady Huntingdon, Seymour, *Life and Times of Selina*, 1:431; also quoted in Tyerman, *Whitefield*, 2:400, 401.

10. William Talbot (1717-1774) of Kineton, Warwickshire and after 1767 at St. Giles, Reading (Cecil/Rouse, *Newton*, 329.

11. George Downing, was rector at Ovington, 1764-1803, Elliott-Binns, *The Early Evangelicals* (1953, Cambridge reprint, 2002), 268, 330.

12. Venn to Lady Huntingdon, Seymour, *Life and Times of Selina*, 1:431; also quoted in Tyerman, *Whitefield*, 2:400, 401.

13. Tyerman, *Whitefield*, 2:400, 401; Thomas Wright, *Town of Cowper* (London, 1886), 102, 103.

Wilberforce (aunt of William Wilberforce).[14] He was converted through Whitefield and became a very wealthy banker and businessperson in London.[15] He was a generous philanthropist and, without Newton asking, he volunteered to provide Newton with additional funds so that the Newtons would not be saddled with expenses for having guests in their vicarage or meeting the needs of the many needy in the area. Indeed, Thornton's pledge was quite generous. 'Be hospitable, and keep an open house for such as are worthy of entertainment—help the poor and needy: I will statedly allow you £200 a year, and readily send whenever you have occasion to draw for more.' And Thornton kept his promise, because over the fifteen and a half years that Newton was in Olney, Thornton had given him upwards of £3,000.[16]

When Newton arrived in Olney, Whitefield was on his sixth mission trip to America (June, 1763 – July, 1765). But as soon as Newton heard that Whitefield had returned, he quickly wrote and asked him to visit Olney. Years before, Whitefield had been unable to accept Newton's invitation to visit Liverpool, but maybe this time Whitefield would be able accept his invitation to Olney. However, Newton did not know that Whitefield had returned exhausted. In fact, as soon as his ship reached Falmouth which was the first harbour on the far southwest coast of England, July 7, 1765, he disembarked and made his way by land. He wrote ahead to the trustees at

---

14. See recent biography, Milton Klein, *An Amazing Grace: John Thornton and the Clapham Sect* (New Orleans, 2004).

15. Cecil/Rouse, *Newton*, 332.

16. Bull, *Newton*, 144.

the Tabernacle asking them to give him time to recover. 'I am very low in body.... Stand, my friends, and insist on my not being brought into action too soon. The poor old shattered bark hath not been in dock one week for a long while.'[17]

Yet despite Whitefield's weakened condition, he sent his reply the same day he received Newton's invitation.[18] He began by affirming Newton's call to pastoral ministry and then responded to the invitation.

Rev. and Dear Sir,

With great pleasure I this day received your kind letter. The contents gladdened my heart. Blessed be God, not only for calling you to the saving knowledge of Himself, but sending you forth also to proclaim the Redeemer's unsearchable riches[19] amongst poor sinners. 'God,' says Dr. Goodwin, 'had but one Son, and He made a minister of Him.' Gladly shall I come whenever bodily strength will allow to join my testimony with yours in Olney pulpit, that God is love.[20]

As yet I have not recovered from the fatigues of my American expedition. My shattered bark is scarce worth docking any more. But I would fain[21] wear [out], and not rust out. Oh! my dear Mr. Newton, indeed and indeed I am ashamed that I have done and suffered so little for Him that hath done and suffered so much for ill

---

17. Quoted in Dallimore, *Whitefield*, 2:455.

18. Diary [2], Friday, 9 Aug. 1765. 'Received a letter from dear Mr. Whitfield* in answer to one I wrote him on Monday.'

19. Ephesians 3:8

20. 1 John 4:8

21. Gladly.

and hell-deserving me. 'Less than the least of all'[22] must be my motto still. Cease not, I entreat you, to pray for me. I am sure my good old friend, Mr. Hull,[23] will join with you. As enabled, you shall both, with all your connections and dear flock, be constantly remembered by, my dear, dear sir,

Yours, etc., etc., in a never-failing Emanuel,
G. Whitefield.
London: August 8, 1765.[24]

As Whitefield indicated, he was too weak to come to Olney. But three months later, Newton received an unexpected offer, which, if he had accepted, would have significantly changed his life and ministry. Furthermore, it would have brought him into formal connection with Whitefield.

A Surprising Offer

In 1740, during Whitefield's second tour in America, he had established an orphanage which he called Bethesda in Georgia, ten miles from Savannah.[25] Subsequently throughout his many tours (both in England and America), he raised substantial funds, including some contributions from his own pocket, to make it succeed. However, during his sixth trip to America he proposed modifying Bethesda to include a college. He had long encouraged education in the colonies and helped raise support for or made personal contributions to Harvard (to rebuild

---

22. Ephesians 3:8

23. Identity unknown.

24. Quoted in Bull, *Newton*, 125, 126.

25. For a recent history see Edward J. Cashin, *Beloved Bethesda: A History of George Whitefield's Home for Boys, 1740-2000* (Macon, 2001).

the 1765 fire-damaged library), the College of New Jersey (later Princeton University), the College of Rhode Island, Wheelock's Indian school (later Dartmouth College), Tennant's Log College, and the Philadelphia Academy (later University of Pennsylvania).[26] To commemorate his work, today a statue of Whitefield stands in a quadrangle at the University of Pennsylvania in Philadelphia.[27] It is the only full statue of him in the world.

In addition, Whitefield was especially concerned that there was 'no seminary for academical* studies as yet founded southward of Virginia.'[28] Typical of Whitefield's large vision, he hoped it would meet the needs of not only Georgia, but also the Carolinas, Florida and the West Indies. Therefore, in 1764 he drew up a document (a 'memorial') and presented it to the Georgia Council. The Council approved, granted an additional 2,000 acres for it and then sent the memorial to England to request a charter from the Privy Council in England. Lord Dartmouth, who was then President of the Board of Trade, presented the venture to the Privy Council. However, because the school was of a religious nature the request was forwarded to the Archbishop of Canterbury. Consequently, when Whitefield returned to England in July he became directly involved in the negotiations. During these ongoing discussions, Lord Dartmouth invited Newton to London

---

26. Lambert, *Pedlar in Divinity*, 208; Dallimore, *Whitefield*, 2:285.

27. This is the statement of Johnston, *Whitefield*, 2:575, who also states that access to this university quadrangle at South 36th and Spruce is restricted, so permission must be granted in advance. For picture, see page 121.

28. Whitefield to Council, quoted in Dallimore, *Whitefield*, 2:434. William and Mary College in Williamsburg, Va., opened in 1694.

so they could discuss a proposal. Understandably, this invitation caught Newton off-guard, especially since he did not know any details. He recorded:

> Sunday [Nov.] 10. My mind through the latter part of the preceding week was much unsettled from a message I received from Lord D desiring to see me. I found myself calm and satisfied with respect to the cause and issue of this business whatever it might be. And yet somehow my intended journey was constantly on my mind. Little foolish things hardly worth the mention are sufficient to employ a world of ungoverned imagination. I had however a good opportunity on Thursday evening.[29] When my journey to London was known, the people [had] much uneasiness and fear lest I should leave them. I am sure it [is] not my intention or desire. Preached in the morning from James 2:10. Afternoon John 3:8. Concluded the evening as usual with the addition of many hearty farewels*, and good wishes for my journey.[30]

---

29. On Thursday evenings he held a gathering for his own church members, as well as many Dissenters. At these he often preached series of expository messages (Hindmarsh, *Newton*, 195). For example from 19 July 1764 to 27 March 1766 he gave seventy-two sermons (which he called lectures) on Romans 8 (Diary [2], 27 March 1766]). On the Thursday mentioned here he preached the first of four sermons on Romans 8: 34. For this sermon see the transcription by Marylynn Rouse, *The Searcher of Hearts* (Christian Focus Publications, Fearn, Ross-shire, 1997), 141-145. Newton kept careful diary notes of his meetings. Uncharacteristically, (but understandable because of the anxiety in his congregation over his trip to London) he did not record his text for that Thursday meeting, but afterwards referred to it in his note on Sunday. The Thursday after he returned from London, he gave his second lecture on this text (Diary [2], 21 Nov. 1765).

30. Diary [2], Sunday, 10 Nov. 1765.

The next morning he set out at six, rode to Dunstable on horseback, continued by post chaise and reached London at three 'safe but wearied.' Despite this, he took the opportunity that evening to attend the Whitefield's Tabernacle where he heard Mr. Kinsman. While there 'saw Mr. W[hitefiel]d and learnt he is partly concerned in my coming up'[31] to London. It seems that Whitefield did not give him any further details of what the meeting with Dartmouth would involve.

The next day he breakfasted with Brewer and heard him preach at Pinner's Hall. After a brief meeting with a Mr. Freeman, he notes, 'proceeded to Lord D., who informed me of the intention of creating a seminary in Georgia, and made me an offer of the Presidentship.*'[32] This was a remarkable proposal. 'I know not what may be the Lord's will but I find no inclination to leave poor Olney, though the offer is great. But unless the Lord calls and clears my way, may I be preserved from listening to the sound of honours and profits. I therefore declined.'[33] That evening he visited his friend Clunie and no doubt shared the startling offer with him.

He quickly sent news to Polly who was anxious to learn the details. 'The secret is out. My first suspicion is right. My Lord [Dartmouth] is the prime manager of Georgia.[34] Mr. Whitefield's orphan-house is to be converted into

---

31. Diary [2], Monday, 11 Nov. 1765.

32. Diary [2], Tuesday, 12 Nov. 1765.

33. Diary [2], Tuesday, 12 Nov. 1765.

34. Dartmouth was President of the Board of Trade (1765, 1766) and later he was appointed Secretary of State for the colonies (1772-1775), Grayson Carter, 'Dartmouth, Earl of, 1731-1801', *DEB*, 292, 293.

a seminary, college, or university; and Mr. Newton is desired to be president thereof, with the annexed living[35] of
Savannah*, the chief town.' He shared his thoughts about
it. 'My love to Olney and your hatred of the water are the
chief reasons which moved me to say I would not accept it,
otherwise it is a most important service.'[36]

Newton had been in Olney only a year-and-a-half and
was enjoying the positive response of the congregation, as
well as attracting others from the area. In fact, the attendance increased so much that a new gallery had to be built
that year to accommodate the worshippers.[37] Hence, it is
understandable that he would want to remain in Olney.
Nevertheless, it appears that despite what he had said to
Polly, he was still processing Dartmouth's offer.

The following morning he breakfasted again with
Brewer. 'Acquainted him with the proposal. He thinks
with me I ought to stay where I am.' From there, he met
with Whitefield. 'We talked the matter over but I was
not altered.' That was Newton's conviction but he still
seemed to leave the door open for his mind to be changed.
'If the Lord would have me [go], I hope he will make my
way clear.' 'That evening he went to hear Whitefield
preach on Acts 17:23. Newton records, 'I heard with
a pleasure; a pleasure and attention beyond what any
man but he can raise. It was thus with me from the time
I first heard him, it is so still.'[38]

---

35. This wording indicates that Newton would also have been a rec-
    tor in Savannah, probably with his living provided by Dartmouth
    as at Olney.

36. Newton to Polly quoted in Bull, *Newton*, 141. Bull says it is in No-
    vember 1765, but does not give the date.

37. Aitken, *Newton*, 189.

38. Diary [2], 13 Nov. 1765.

Newton filled the next day meeting various acquaintances including Dr. Andrew Gifford,[39] the pastor of Eagle Street Baptist church and noted collector of rare theological books. Then on Friday 'waited on my Lord [Dartmouth], confirmed my former sentiment and took leave.' Later that day he dined with William Romaine and preached at the Lock chapel where Martin Madan served. On Saturday, he returned to Olney after eight active and eventful days. Though tired from the emotionally draining journey, he preached twice that Sunday. He admitted afterwards that doing this was difficult. 'My foolish thoughts run upon the occasion of my late journey. I hope I have done with it, my choice (if the Lord please*) is fixed, but my roving vain imagination is beyond my controul.*'[40] Despite this, the service went well. And he records that the evening meeting was 'full as usual; the people seem well pleased with my return' and added 'and I hope I am so likewise.'

Tuesday was the regular church prayer meeting and he spoke on Isaiah 49:16 'Behold, I have graven thee upon the palms of my hands; thy walls are continually before me.' Possibly through preparing that message he received the reassurance he needed. That evening he gave his final answer. 'Wrote to L.D. my deliberate thoughts on the proposed affair – which I heartily decline.'[41]

---

39. Diary [2], 14 Nov. 1765. Because of his knowledge of rare books (he owned a rare first edition of the Tyndale New Testament), Gifford (1700-1784) also served as assistant librarian of the British Library (E. F. Clipson, 'Gifford, Andrew, 1700-1784', *DEB*, 438).

40. Diary [2], Sunday, 17 Nov. 1765.

41. Diary [2], 19 Nov. 1765.

Newton's decision proved to be the correct one, because ultimately Whitefield's desire to establish a college did not materialise. The Archbishop of Canterbury required the school president be a clergy from the Established Church and that the school be operated as a Church of England institution. He refused to budge. By contrast, from Whitefield's perspective, the president would probably be a clergy from the Established Church (as Newton was), but he did not want it to be a requirement for the college to be governed that way because the majority of colonists were Dissenters and had given significant funds over the years for the orphanage. In the end, Whitefield turned again to the Georgia Council to give their support for a modified proposal of a public academy attached to the orphanage. In this way, Whitefield said 'beloved Bethesda will not only be continued as a house of mercy for poor orphans, but will be confirmed as a seat and nursery of sound learning and religious education.'[42] They approved and construction started. But in 1773, two-and-a-half years after Whitefield's death, the main building was destroyed in an electrical storm, in 1782 the whole property was confiscated in the American Revolution (1775-1783) and by 1800 a visitor observed there was no school of any kind.[43]

---

42. Tyerman, *Whitefield*, 2:528.

43. Tyerman, *Whitefield*, 2:528, 584, 585. Today the Bethesda Academy, as it is called, is a private school for about 120 boys (grades six to twelve), forty of whom are in residence. Therefore, some of Whitefield's hopes for Bethesda continue to this day. The webpage for the Academy proudly states that it is 'the oldest child caring institution in the country.' On the 650 acre property sits Whitefield Chapel that has a 135 seating capacity.

Ongoing Connections with Whitefield Supporters

It is interesting to note that when Newton was in London to meet with Whitefield and Lord Dartmouth to discuss the Georgia college proposal, he also had breakfast with Mr. and Mrs. West. Daniel West Esq. (d.1796) was one of the trustees of the Moorfields Tabernacle and Tottenham Court Road chapel.[44] Newton's diary mentions that earlier he met Mrs. West at the home of John Collett Ryland (1723-1792) in Northampton, about ten miles northwest of Olney.[45] There Ryland, who admired Whitefield and endorsed his ministry, served as pastor of College Lane Baptist Church and also had a boys' boarding school.[46] Mrs. Trinder, another member of the congregation, had a girls' boarding school. These two schools were well respected and drew many students; some far beyond the town. For example, Ignatius, the son of Benjamin Ingham (1712 – 1772) the great evangelist in Yorkshire in the north and nephew of Lady Huntingdon, attended this school.[47] Some came from London. The Wests had one son, Daniel Jr., at Ryland's school and so did Samuel Brewer.[48] Some of Captain Clunie's

---

44. Diary [2], 14 Nov. 1765. See Bull, *Newton*, 140 and Bull, *Letters of John Newton with biographical sketches*, 126.

45. As mentioned in Bull, *Newton*, 140.

46. See Peter Naylor, 'John Collett Ryland (1723-1792),' in Michael Haykin, ed., *The British Particular Baptists 1638-1910*, 3 vols., (Springfield, 1998-2003), 1:184-201 and Bruce Hindmarsh, *The English Conversion Narrative* (Oxford, 2005), 301-320.

47. For details of Ryland's school and his connection with Whitefield, see Gordon, 'A Revealing Unpublished Letter of George Whitefield to John Collett Ryland.'

48. Gordon, *Wise Counsel*, 64, n.2, 3.

children also attended.[49] These are referred to in Newton's letters to Clunie. 'Mr. Ryland sends me word that he expects Mr. and Mrs. West will be at Northampton by this day fortnight and that you propose to accompany them. I have some thoughts of meeting you there on Monday the 19th to escort you all to Olney.'[50] Again, to Captain and Mrs. Clunie he wrote, 'We long to see you both; we left your children and Master West well this morning at Northampton. May the Lord bless them all and give them to know and love their parents' God.'[51] About eight years later, John and Polly enrolled their adopted orphan niece in the girl's school. Newton regularly visited with Ryland and spoke at the two schools in Northampton. This school connection reveals one of the many networks of those who endorsed the ongoing Evangelical Revival.

Through various networks, they assisted one another, despite their individual denominational allegiances. For example, Brewer, though he was pastor of the large Stepney Congregational chapel, often spoke at the Tuesday society meeting at the West's home in London. Clunie attended this too.[52] There is record of Polly attending this meeting when she visited London and Newton spoke there on one occasion, in place of Brewer.[53] Newton and the Wests corresponded for many years and they visited

---

49. Newton to Clunie, 16 May 1765, Newton (Clunie), 164, 165.

50. Newton to Clunie, 4 Aug. 1765, Newton (Clunie), 82.

51. Newton to Clunie, 16 May 1767, Newton (Clunie), 164, 165.

52. Newton to Clunie, 9 Feb. 1766, Newton (Clunie), 95.

53. Bull, *Newton*, 152, 173.

back and forth.[54] Years later, Newton collected twenty-one of his letters to Mr. and Mrs. West that he included in his sequel *to Cardiphonia*.[55]

Whenever possible, Newton connected with Whitefield while visiting friends in London. For example, a year after turning down the offer to go to Georgia, when Newton and Polly travelled to London primarily to see Brewer who was confined because of leg pain, his visits included Whitefield. He had 'several pleasant hours' visiting friends at Clapham, including his philanthropist friend John Thornton. Wednesday forenoon he heard Romaine preach and that evening went to hear Whitefield preach from 2 Cor. 5:14.[56] The following year he was back in London to respond to Thornton's offer of a church in Cottenham, Cambridgeshire. While there, he heard Whitefield preach from Judges 8:4 and dined with him the next day at Mr. West's.[57] In the end, Newton turned down the offer and returned to Olney. Lord Dartmouth 'expressed much satisfaction' at Newton's desire 'in conscience' to remain with the Olney congregation. Newton admitted that had he moved he would have 'sunk under the weight of a broken heart. [and] Now it is over I can bless the

---

54. For example, after John and Polly's visit to London in August 1766, the Wests returned with them to Olney where they stayed for about a week.

55. *Works*, 6:59-111 (letters to West are dated 25 Jan. 1766 - 3 May 1776).

56. Diary [2], 10 Aug. 1766.

57. Diary [1767], 18, 19 Feb. 1767. Transcription of this MS diary provided by Marylynn Rouse. He expands on this visit in his quick letter reporting back to Polly, 19 Feb. 1767 (David M. Rubenstein Library Rare Book & Manuscript Library, Duke University).

Lord for having knit me and my dear people so close in mutual affection.'[58]

Whitefield's Sudden Death

Newton continued to invite Whitefield to Olney. In 1769 he mentioned this to Captain Clunie. 'I wrote to Mr. Whitfield* last week, but have not had an answer; perhaps my letter came when he was all in a hurry, and upon the point of departure. May the Lord go with him, and bless him wherever he is led.'[59] Indeed Whitefield was busy because three days before Newton sent the letter, he had sailed (4 Sept. 1769) on what would be his final voyage to America. Sadly, a little over a year later, on 30 September 1770, at the age of fifty-five, Whitefield died suddenly of an asthma attack in Newburyport, Massachusetts. He was buried there in the vault of the Presbyterian Church. The abrupt end had come for this great trans-Atlantic preacher. Arnold Dallimore concludes his moving biography of Whitefield this way: 'So passed from this life the mighty preacher, the great evangelist, the man of God, George Whitefield. Throughout the long years of labour and many months of weakness he had lived to preach Christ, but now, as earth receded and heaven opened, he "died to be with him," to join the redeemed host who sing His praises before the throne.'[60]

Whitefield had written his last will and testament just six months before he died.[61] Among the details, he

---

58. Quoted in Bull, *Newton*, 155.

59. Newton to Clunie, 7 Sept. 1769, Newton (Clunie), 188.

60. Dallimore, *Whitefield*, 2:506.

61. See full deed dated, 22 March 1770, Gillies, *Whitefield*, 290-294.

expressed his fond feelings for John and Charles Wesley. It was customary to have mourning rings made and given to a few close friend or associates. Therefore, he willed that six be made; with one to each of his four executors. The other two were for the Wesley brothers. He explained, 'I leave a mourning ring to my honoured and dear friends and disinterested[62] fellow-labourers, the Rev. Messrs. John and Charles Wesley, in token of my indissoluble union with them, in heart and Christian affection, notwithstanding our difference in judgment about some particular points of doctrine. Grace be with all them, of whatever denomination, that love our Lord Jesus, our common Lord, in sincerity'[63]

Before he had set out from England for this trip to America, he had requested Robert Keen, one of his trustees at the Tabernacle, that if he should die, he wanted John Wesley to preach his funeral sermon.[64] The problem now was that Whitefield's funeral came at a very awkward time. At the annual Methodist Conference in London about two months earlier, Wesley had made statements that caused uproar with the leading Calvinists, including Lady Huntingdon.[65] When the conference minutes became public it led to a bitter conflict between the two Methodists groups and became known as the Minutes Controversy. Nevertheless, to the credit of both the

---

62. Impartial. Frank Lambert, *Pedlar in Divinity*, 214, indicates that usage of this word at the time 'suggests a motivation aimed at advancing public rather than private interests.'

63. Gillies, *Whitefield*, 294.

64. Dallimore, *Whitefield*, 2:510.

65. John R. Tyson with Boyd S. Schlenther, *In the Midst of Early Methodism: Lady Huntingdon and Her Correspondence* (Plymouth, UK, 2006), 11.

trustees and John Wesley they followed through with Whitefield's final request.

Consequently, on 18 November 1770 John Wesley preached at Tottenham Court Road chapel and later that Sunday, repeated the sermon at the Tabernacle in Moor-fields. The sermon was largely an historical sketch of Whitefield's life and a tribute to some of his strengths in-cluding zeal, tender-heartedness, eloquence and power of persuasion. For the occasion, Charles Wesley composed a hymn. Four lines of the first verse stated:

> Servant of God, well done!
> Thy glorious warfare's past,
> The battle's fought, the race is won,
> And thou art crown'd at last;[66]

Numerous pastors in America and England preached ser-mons commemorating the death of Whitefield. John New-ton did on 11 November 1770 and chose John 5:35 as his text, 'He was a burning and a shining light.'[67] Soon after White-field died, John Gillies who was his close friend in Glasgow, collected and published the six-volume *The Works of the Rev-erend George Whitefield* (London, 1771-1772) and *Memoirs of the Life of the Rev. George Whitefield* (London, 1772). These contain valuable source material. Fortunately, Gillies included what he called an 'extract' of Newton's sermon in the *Mem-oirs*. It does not appear to have been published before and it is not known how Gillies, in Scotland, obtained a copy of it. In the *Memoirs* he specifically lists titles of eight published

---

66. *Works of Wesley*, 5:167-182 (Grand Rapids, 2002) cited in Johnston, *Whitefield*, 2:477.

67. Newton used this verse also to describe several other preachers, including Conyers, Hill, Grimshaw and Colonel Gardiner.

funeral sermons, including those by John Wesley and Henry Venn.[68] But Newton is not in the list. In fact, Gillies separately describes Newton's extract as a '*manuscript funeral sermon*' (emphasis added).[69] Probably, someone sent him a copy that Newton had sent to a colleague. Most likely this was Daniel West, Newton's friend and one of Whitefield's trustees. West would have been in contact with Gillies, who was gathering the Whitefield material for publication. It is known that Newton did send a copy to at least one person. This was Joshua Symonds, pastor of the Bunyan Meeting House in nearby Bedford. In his cover letter, Newton writes, 'Last Lord's-day evening, I preached to a very large auditory, on occasion of Mr. Whitefield's death... . I have sent you what I wrote of my sermon, and which (so far as it goes) is nearly verbatim the same with what I spoke from the pulpit.'[70] And with the funeral message still fresh on his heart, he added a closing concluding remark. 'Well, he is now at rest: he is now with the Lord whom he loved! He was always desirous of a sudden death, and the Lord indulged him with it. He is rejoicing, but his removal is lamented by thousands, and seems a heavy blow to those who were more immediately connected with him. He was much beloved at Olney, and had been a great blessing to me. I, therefore, thought it incumbent on me to bear my public testimony to him.'[71]

The extract of this sermon has not been published in full since 1772, when Gillies included it in the *Memoirs*.

---

68. Gillies, *Whitefield*, 620, 621.

69. Gillies, *Whitefield* , xix.

70. Newton to Joshua Symonds, 16 Nov. 1770, ALS is MS 00263 (Emory Family Papers) in Fisher Rare Book Library, University of Toronto. A major portion also published in *Baptist Magazine* (1817): 371.

71. Newton to Joshua Symonds, 16 Nov. 1770.

Therefore, because it is quite insightful and reveals New-ton's value of Whitefield, it is now provided here in full as it appeared in *Memoirs*.[72]

'Some ministers are burning and shining lights in a pe-culiar and eminent degree. Such a one, I doubt not, was the servant of God whose death we now lament. I have had some opportunities of looking over the History of the Church in past ages,[73] and I am not backward to say, that I have not read or heard of any person, since the Apos-tles' days, of whom it may more emphatically be said, 'He was a burning and a shining light,' than the late Mr. *Whitefield*, whether we consider the warmth of his zeal, the greatness of his ministerial talents, or the extensive usefulness with which the Lord honoured him. I do not mean to praise the man, but the Lord, who furnished him, and made him what he was. He was raised up to shine in a dark place. The state of religion, when he first ap-peared in public, was very low in our Established Church. I speak the truth, though to some it may be an offensive truth. The doctrines of Grace, were seldom heard from the pulpit, and the life and power of godliness were little known. Many of the most spiritual among the Dissent-ers, were mourning under the sense of a great spreading declension on their side. What a change has taken place throughout the land within a little more than thirty years, that is, since the time when the first set of despised min-isters came from *Oxford*! and how much of this change has been owing to God's blessing on Mr. *Whitefield*'s labors,* is

---

72. Gillies, *Whitefield*, 341-346.

73. He had recently written *Review of Ecclesiastical History* (London, 1769) that covered the first century of church history. See *Works* 3: 2-297. This work inspired Joseph Milner to complete the his-tory (*The History of the Church of* Christ (London, 1794 -1797).

well known to many who have lived through this period; and can hardly be denied by those who are least willing to allow it.

First[ly], He was a *burning* light. He had an ardent zeal for GOD, [and] an enflamed desire for the salvation of sinners. So that no labours could weary him, no difficulties or opposition discourage him, hardly any limits could confine him; not content with the bounds of a county, or a kingdom, this messenger of good tidings preached the everlasting Gospel in almost every considerable place in *England*, *Scotland* and *Ireland*, and throughout the British empire in *America*, which is an extent of more than a thousand miles. Most of these places he visited again and again; nor did he confine his attention to places of note, but in the former part of his ministry, was ready to preach to few, as well as to many, wherever a door was opened; though in the latter part of his life, his frequent illness, and the necessity of his more immediate charge,[74] confined him more at home. In some of his most early excursions, the good Providence of God led him here,[75] and many, I trust, were made willing to rejoice in his light, and have reason to bless God, that ever they saw and heard him.

Secondly, He was *shining* light: his zeal was not like wildfire, but directed by sound principles, and a sound judgment. In this part of his character, I would observe,

1st[ly]. Though he was very young, when he came out, the Lord soon gave him a very clear view of the Gospel. In the sermons he published soon after his first

---

74. The Tabernacle and the Chapel in London.
75. As mentioned earlier, in 1739 he first preached in Olney with significant results.

appearance, there is the same evangelical strain observable, as in those which he preached in his advanced years. Time and observation, what he felt, and what he saw, enlarged his experience, and gave his preaching an increasing ripeness and favour, as he grew older in the work; but from first to last he preached the same Gospel, and was determined to know nothing but *Jesus Christ*, and him crucified.

2dly, His steadiness and perseverance in the truth was the more remarkable, considering the difficulties and snares he was sometimes beset with. But the Lord kept him steady, so that neither the example, nor friendship, nor importunity[76] of those he dearly loved, were capable of moving him.

3rdly. The Lord gave him manner of preaching, which was peculiarly his own. He copied from none, and I never met any one who could imitate him with success. They who attempted, generally made themselves disagreeable.[77] His familiar address, the power of his action, his marvellous talent in fixing the attention even of the most careless, I need not describe to those who have heard him, and to those who have not, the attempt would be vain. Other ministers could, perhaps, preach the Gospel as clearly and in general say the same things, but, I believe, no man living could say them in his way. Here I always thought him unequalled, and I hardly expect to see his equal while I live.

4th[ly]. But that which finished his character as a shining light, and is now his crown of rejoicing, was the

---

76. Insistence, begging.

77. Displeasing, offensive.

singular success which the Lord was pleased to give him in winning souls; what numbers entered the Kingdom of Glory before him, and what numbers are now lamenting his loss, who were awakened by his ministry? It seemed as if he never preached in vain. Perhaps there is hardly a place, in all the extensive compass of his labours, where some may not be found who thankfully acknowledge him as their spiritual father. Nor was he an awakening preacher only wherever he came; if he preached but a single discourse, he usually brought a season of refreshment and revival with him to those who had already received the truth. Great as his immediate and personal usefulness was, his occasional[78] usefulness (if I may so call it) was perhaps much greater. Many have cause to be thankful for him, who never saw or heard him. I have already observed, that there was something peculiar in his manner of preaching, in which no person of sound judgment would venture to imitate him. But notwithstanding this, he was in other respects, a signal and happy pattern and model for preachers. He introduced a way of close and lively application to the conscience, for which I believe many of the most admired and eminent preachers now living, will not be ashamed, or unwilling to acknowledge themselves his debtors.'

This was Newton's perspective in 1770 and it clearly shows that he had carefully noticed the unique aspects of Whitefield's powerful ministry. In his will Whitefield had made Daniel West Esq. and Robert Keen joint trustees of the Moorfields Tabernacle and Tottenham Court

---

78. The context shows Newton is using one of the meanings of *occasional* as being *secondary*.

Road chapel and two of the four executors.[79] In a letter to West, Newton expressed his prayer that the ministry of the 'two great houses' (Tabernacle and Chapel) over which West was co-trustee, would continue to flourish. 'We were glad to hear of your welfare, and of the prosperity with which the Lord favours you at home and in the two great houses; which, I hope, will continue to be like trees planted by the waters of the sanctuary, maintaining the leaves of the Gospel doctrine always green and flourishing, and abounding with a constant succession of blossoms, green and ripe fruit; I mean believers in the states of babes, young men and fathers in Christ.'[80] This was about a year-and-a-half after the death of Whitefield.

A few months later, while visiting in a home, Newton came across a volume of Whitefield's sermons published by Joseph Gurney. Without Whitefield's permission, Gurney had taken these down 'verbatim in shorthand and faithfully transcribed' them (as claimed on the title page). Gurney's volume of eighteen sermons came out in 1771. But prior to this, a few single sermons were released. When Whitefield saw these, he denounced them. 'It is not verbatim,' he complained, 'in some places Mr. Gurney makes me to speak false accord, and even nonsense.'[81] After Whitefield's death the executors followed Whitefield's assessment and refused to include these eighteen sermons in the official collection of his sermons. Hence, Gillies' *Works of Whitefield* ('printed under the direction of his

---

79. Philip, *Whitefield*, 569; Tyerman, *Whitefield*, 2:609. For brief biography of West, see Bull, *Letters of John Newton with biographical sketches*, 126.

80. *Works* 6:88 (2 June 1772).

81. Quoted in Tyerman, *Whitefield* 2:461.

executors')[82]contains only fifty-seven sermons, and none
from Gurney's pen.[83] Despite Gurney's transcriptions not
being authorised by Whitefield, Newton could not resist
perusing the little volume. 'I have read several of them,' he
informed West (one of the four executors who blocked
the endorsement of these sermons), 'They are, indeed,
more loose and inaccurate than printed sermons usually are.' Though having acknowledged this limitation, he
saw some value in them. 'I think them the more valuable
in one respect on this account that they give a lively idea
of his manner of preaching, which can hardly be guessed
at from the sermons formerly printed in his name.' These
sermons transcribed by Gurney touched Newton and
brought back fond memories. 'I cannot read a page, but
I seem to have the man before my eyes. His voice, his ges-
ture, every particular, returns to my memory, as if I heard
him but yesterday.'[84]

Newton served faithfully in Olney for almost sixteen
years. He spent many afternoons visiting his flock in
their homes and was therefore much appreciated for his
pastoral care. His services and meetings became known

---

82. Gillies, *Whitefield Works*, 1:i.

83. The sermons are in vols. 5 and 6. These sermons have now been
slightly revised and published, along with four others, in Lee Gatiss,
ed., *The Sermons of George Whitefield*, 2 vols. (Wheaton, Ill., 2012).

84. *Works* 6:94 (14 September 1772). Newton tells us that on a visit
to London, he went to see a 'resemblance of Whitefield in wax'
(Diary [2], 14 Aug. 1772). 'A collection of wax figures in New York
City (a precursor to Madame Tussauds) contained a life-size
likeness of Whitefield. The proprietor of the museum, Patience
Wright, took the image to London for display after the revival-
ist's death, along with statues of Benjamin Franklin and David
Garrick.' Kidd, *Whitefield*, 254.

for their singing. Newton carefully searched for hymns that reinforced his sermon texts. To aid this he collected 'sets of texts with suitable verses from *Watts' Hymns*, etc.' When he could not find a suitable hymn, he wrote one. 'I am sometimes forced to write a few lines myself when I cannot suit the text from the books I have.'[85] Consequently he composed many hymns and William Cowper, when he moved to Olney to be near Newton, joined him in this effort. Eventually, in 1779, Newton collected these and published them in a three volume set called *Olney Hymns*. The uniqueness of this hymnbook is that all were written by them (281 by Newton and 67 by Cowper). Today among the best known of Cowper's are *There is a fountain filled with blood* and *God moves in a mysterious way*. For Newton these would include, *How sweet the name of Jesus sounds*, *Glorious things of thee are spoken*, and of course, *Amazing Grace*. As stated in his hymn-book preface, the hymns were written with the 'desire of promoting the faith and comfort of sincere Christians.'[86] This hymnbook became quite popular and went through many editions.

---

85. Diary [2], 31 Oct. 1765. Here he mentions that he planned on printing this compilation, though I am unaware of this ever being published. His hymnbook was divided in three sections: 141 on biblical texts, 100 on topics (seasons, ordinances, providences, creation), and 107 on aspects of the Christian life (including comfort, surrender, etc.).

86. *Olney Hymns*, in *Works* 3: 201.

6

Ministry In London (1780-1807)

Sharing Fond Memories of Whitefield.

In 1780, Newton accepted John Thornton's generous offer to serve as rector of St. Mary Woolnoth in the heart of London's financial district. There, for twenty-eight years, Newton would have a significant ministry to his new congregation and beyond. This included advising influential evangelical pastors and statesmen (e.g., William Wilberforce), entering the fight against slavery by publishing *Thoughts upon the African Slave Trade* (1788) and twice standing before parliamentary committees to speak against it. In addition he helped form a small fortnightly discussion group, called the *Eclectic Society*, of select pastors and leading laymen. He also actively promoted the cause of missions and humanitarian efforts.

In many ways, Newton became something of an elder statesman in the evangelical world (being twenty years older than the other members of the *Eclectic Society*). He was a bridge between the early evangelicals (Lady Huntingdon, Grimshaw, Romaine, John and Charles Wesley, Whitefield) and the next generation (William Wilberforce, Charles Simeon, William Jay). Because he had both heard Whitefield publicly and talked with him privately, it was natural for others (who had not the same privilege) to ask him about Whitefield. The following are

Newton's comments (the first three are in chronological order) about Whitefield.

1)   1784 – Speaking of himself, Newton said, 'I believe no minister can be more comfortable and happy with his people than I am.' To illustrate this he commented, 'Mr. Whitfield* used to call his pulpit his throne.' Applying this personally, Newton continued. 'When I am upon my throne, I can look down upon the poets, philosophers, artists, archbishops, cardinals, popes, and kings of the earth with pity. If they know not my Lord and Saviour, they are to be pitied indeed. I would not exchange the honour of proclaiming his glory and grace, and preaching his gospel to sinners a single day, for a whole life of what they account the best and the greatest.'[1] Newton's church was in a prominent place in the centre of London. Because the mayor's official residence was in the parish, he was expected to attend at least once a year.

2)   1794 – Newton was describing John Berridge of Everton who had a very effective ministry, though he could not break his habit of making humorous statements in the pulpit that at times were crude ('his taste was far from delicate ... low and vulgar') even to his friends. Then Newton's thoughts turned to Whitefield whose use of humour in the pulpit was unique. 'Mr. Whitfield* likewise could say comical things; but then it was in a manner quite his own, in which none of his imitators could succeed. When he made his hearers smile, it was usually with a design to make them weep, and I have more than

1.   Newton to William Bull, 6 Dec. 1784, in T. P. Bull, ed., *One Hundred and Twenty Nine Letters from the Rev. John Newton to the Rev. William Bull* (London, 1847), 203.

once seen these different effects produced in almost the same minute.'[2]

3)   1795 – William Wilberforce recorded, 'Old Newton breakfasted with me. He talked in the highest terms of Whitefield as by far the greatest preacher he had ever known.'[3]

4)   Newton cautioned, 'Good men have need to take heed of building upon groundless impressions. Mr. [George] Whitefield had a son, whom he imagined born to be a very extraordinary man; but the son died, and the father was cured of his mistake.'[4] This refers to the statement Whitefield made at his baby boy's baptism. He declared before the thousand gathered that his son would grow up to 'be a preacher of the everlasting gospel' and therefore named him John, after John the Baptist. But when the little boy died, it humbled Whitefield who realised his error and admitted that he had misapplied scripture. He saw that he had wrongly 'hoped that he was to be great in the sight of God.'[5]

5)   Historian Seymour comments, 'Few preachers possessed eloquence so well adapted to an auditory as Mr. Whitefield. His metaphors were drawn from sources

---

2.   John Newton to John Campbell, 1 Aug., 1794, Seattle Pacific University Library, Special Collections, ‹ http://digitalcommons. spu.edu/cgi/viewcontent.cgi?article=1028&context=newton_campbell›[accessed 26 July, 2015]. Berridge's identity was not disclosed in the published edition by John Campbell, ed., *Letters and Conversational Remarks of the Rev. John Newton* (London, 1808), 35.

3.   Samuel Wilberforce, *The Life of William Wilberforce* (revised and condensed from original edition, London, 1768), 133.

4.   *Works* 1:103.

5.   Dallimore, *Whitefield*, 2: 167; Tyerman, *Whitefield*, 2:85, 86.

easily understood by his hearers, and frequently from the circumstances of the moment. The application was generally happy, and sometimes rose to the true sublime: for he was a man of warm imagination and by no means devoid of taste.'[6] To support this claim he quotes a comment Newton made in a breakfast conversation with 'noblemen and gentlemen,' when the topic of powerful preachers came up. Newton said:

> 'I bless God that I have lived in his time; many were the winter mornings I have got up at four, to attend his Tabernacle discourses at five: and I have seen Moor- fields as full of lanterns at these times as I suppose the Haymarket[7] is full of flambeaux[8] on an Opera night. As a preacher, if any man was to ask me who was the second I ever had heard, I should be at some loss; but in regard to the first, Mr. Whitefield exceeded so far every other man of my time, that I should be at none. He was the original of popular preaching, and all our popular ministers are only his copies."[9]

'As a proof of the power' of Mr. Whitefield's preaching, Seymour includes three examples that Newton gave. The first was of 'an officer at Glasgow, who had heard him preach, laid a wager with another, that at a certain char- ity sermon, though he went with prejudice, he would be compelled to give something; the other, to make sure, laid all the money out of his pockets,[10] but before he left the

---

6. Seymour, *The Life and Times of Selina*, 1:91.

7. Haymarket was part of the theatre district in the West End of London.

8. Flaming torches.

9. Seymour, *The Life and Times of Selina*, 1:92.

10. In other words, he emptied his pockets before he went to hear Whitefield.

church, he was glad to borrow some, and lose his bet.' The second illustrated Whitefield's persuasive power. 'After one sermon, he raised *six hundred pounds* for the inhabitants of a village in Germany that had been plundered by Russian troops. After the sermon, Mr. Whitefield said, "We shall sing a hymn, during which those who do not choose to give their mite on this aw[e]ful occasion may sneak off." No one moved and he got out of the pulpit ordered all the doors to be shut but one. He then stood at that door, at which he held the plate himself, and collected the above sum.' The third was that from Whitefield's preaching, 'in one week he received not fewer than a thousand letters from persons distressed in their consciences by the energy of his preaching.'[11]

This response of a thousand letters may sound exaggerated. However, Whitefield said something similar.[12] In May 1742, when he saw about ten thousand revellers gathered at Moorfields for public amusement, he placed his field pulpit at the side of the clearing and began to preach. Many gathered around the pulpit and the boisterous crowd became 'hushed and solemn.' Encouraged by this, he returned to preach that afternoon to a much larger crowd. They were attentive, though there were some disruptions, especially from the heckling entertainers who lost their audiences and profits. Despite the noise and 'a few stones, dirt, rotten eggs, and pieces of dead cats' thrown at him, he saw, as he put it, 'the lion-like

---

11. Seymour, *The Life and Times of Selina*, 1:92. I have been unable to determine where Seymour found these comments by Newton.

12. Though Newton says 'in one week' and Whitefield describes an event that took place in one day, it is possible both are referring to the same event.

crowd turned into lambs.' At the end, he announced he would return that evening to preach again. The response to his evening sermon was remarkable, even though there were organised attempts by some to disrupt the sermon. Afterwards, with his pockets 'full of notes from persons brought under concern,' he and members of his congregation returned to the Tabernacle nearby. There he read many of these notes to the congregation and they rejoiced, 'That so many sinners were snatched, in such an unexpected, unlikely place and manner, out of the very jaws of the devils.' Whitefield estimated that 'three hundred and fifty souls were received in one day, and I believe the number of notes exceeded a thousand.'[13]

Those were some of the fond memories that Newton had of Whitefield. He had been privileged to meet and hear Whitefield numerous times and become one of his friends. Like Whitefield, Newton ministered faithfully to the end. However, some of Newton's friends were concerned for him when he turned eighty and had failing health and eyesight. Hence they encouraged him to refrain from preaching. To that he responded, 'What! Shall the old blasphemer stop while can speak?'[14] He died 31 Dec. 1807 at the age of eighty-two and was buried at St. Mary Woolnoth, London, where he had served twenty-eight years.

He wrote his own epitaph that summarised his life, his service in Olney and London, and his marriage to Mary.

---

13. Whitefield to 'Mr. L', 11 May 1742, in Haykin, *The Revived Puritan*, 147-151. Letter is also in *Whitefield Works*, 1: 384-386. This gathering is portrayed in the famous painting 'Whitefield preaching at Moorfields, 1742' by Eyre Crowe (1824-1910) in 1865 and in an engraving of it the same year. See page 119.

14. Cecil/Rouse, *Newton*, 164.

JOHN NEWTON
CLERK[15]
ONCE AN INFIDEL AND LIBERTINE
A SERVANT OF SLAVES IN AFRICA
WAS
BY THE RICH MERCY
OF OUR LORD AND SAVIOUR
JESUS CHRIST
PRESERVED, RESTORED, PARDONED
AND APPOINTED TO PREACH THE FAITH
HE HAD LONG LABORED TO DESTROY.

///////////

HE MINISTERED
NEAR XVI YEARS AS CURATE AND VICAR
OF OLNEY IN BUCKS,
AND XXVIII AS RECTOR
OF THESE UNITED PARISHES[16].

//////

ON FEB[RY] THE FIRST HE MARRIED
MARY
DAUGHTER OF THE LATE GEORGE CATLETT,
OF CHATHAM, KENT
WHOM HE RESIGNED
TO THE LORD WHO GAVE HER
ON DEC[R] THE XVTH MDCCXC[17]

---

15. An eighteenth century word for clergy (Johnson's *Dictionary*, rev. ed.,1768).

16. When the Great Fire in London, 1666, destroyed the nearby church, *St. Mary Woolchurch Haw*, that parish was joined with that of *St. Mary Woolnoth*, hence the term 'United Parishes.'

17. Bull, *Newton*, 360. For picture of this marble epitaph in St. Mary Woolnoth, see Aitken, *Newton*, plate 7.

7

Whitefield's Impact on Newton

We have followed Newton on his journey, especially after he quit the sea November 1754. Let us now review how Whitefield influenced (both directly and indirectly) Newton. Prior to Newton conversing at length with Captain Clunie in the St. Kitts harbour that year, he was surprisingly unaware of the theological/denominational issues and the growing Evangelical Revival. He admitted years later that he had been a solitary Christian. However, that all changed during his ten months of unemployment when he took frequent trips from Chatham to immerse himself in the dynamic spiritual life in and around London. It was during this time that he became committed to an evangelical Calvinism, especially as embodied in George Whitefield.

WHITEFIELD'S DIRECT IMPACT ON NEWTON

Through Whitefield's Public Ministry

One cannot imagine what it must have been like for Newton, after seven years being an isolated Christian, to suddenly experience the vibrant life in the London church services and mid-week meetings during the Evangelical Revival. Much was happening and he had heard about Whitefield, but not heard him. As soon as he learned that Whitefield had returned to London, he quickly dropped everything to go back to the city. His goal was not only to hear Whitefield but also to meet with him. As he went, he sought divine guidance for the journey, 'I pray that the Lord will direct my steps and direct my conversation to my good and his glory'.[1] In his *An Authentic Narrative* he fondly looked back on that first week of hearing Whitefield. 'Though I had little personal acquaintance with him till afterwards, his ministry was *exceedingly useful to me* [emphasis added].'[2] He was disappointed that he was able to meet Whitefield for only three very brief times (July 6, 7), the longest being five minutes. But the opportunity to see and hear Whitefield preach made up for that because his sermons deeply impacted him.

His Preaching

He first had the joy to hear this great evangelist in early June 1755 at the Tabernacle in London. Newton was overwhelmed with Whitefield's oratorical power and evangelistic passion. A few weeks after Newton moved to Liverpool, Whitefield arrived and ended up staying for a five-day preaching mission. This time Newton was privileged to hear him further, have conversations with him and correspond with him afterwards. Newton's diary notes and letters that we have examined indicate that Newton heard Whitefield preach twenty times over a span of twelve years. The documents we have reviewed show that he heard him six times in London, nine during his visit to Liverpool,

---

1. Diary [1] 5 June 1755.
2. Letter 14 (2 Feb. 1763), *An Authentic Narrative*, 90. Note that in the 1998 reprint (Hindmarsh, ed., *The Life and Spirituality of John Newton*), letters 13 and 14 are incorrectly dated 1764.

and later on five separate occasions in London. Probably there were other times as well, but are unknown because there are gaps in Newton's diary.[3] On hearing Whitefield ten years after that first time, Newton expressed his appreciation of Whitefield's preaching. 'I heard him with pleasure; a pleasure and attention beyond what any man but he can raise. It was thus with me from the time I first heard him, it is so still.'[4]

After Newton returned home from first hearing Whitefield in London, he transferred his notes into his diary, sat and debriefed. He praised God for the privilege of hearing Whitefield. More than that, he committed himself to be willing to publicly acknowledge his admiration of him, whom he had earlier described to Polly as 'this persecuted despised man'.[5] He was now firmly determined to stand up for 'his vindication' and to endure 'any kind of reproach' that he himself might experience for doing so. Two days later, he took a long meditative walk, which was his custom, and thanked God that his time in London had been 'a week of continual feasting.'[6]

It is revealing that Newton did not give details or headings of the first five sermons he heard. Instead, he recorded 'striking thoughts' (sermon one). He probably

---

3. For example, there is almost a four year gap in Diary [2]. During most of 1767-1771 he stopped writing in this large diary and instead 'kept brief account of the principal events that have occurred, in several pocket books.' (Diary [2], 1 Jan. 1772).

4. Diary, [2], Nov. 13, 1765.

5. As stated in his earlier letter to his wife (no date) MS 2935 (f. 218) at Lambeth Palace.

6. Diary [1] 12, 14 June 1755

was too overwhelmed. He informed Polly that sermon five 'exceeded all the rest and really was beyond [his] imagination.' But by the sixth sermon, which was the final one he heard that week, he mentioned the headings and included further detail. When Whitefield visited Liverpool, Newton's diary notes are expanded. This time he provides the headings. He confessed that generally he could not include more. For example, of sermon eight he said, 'I can only mention some of the heads, the power and substance of his discourses are not to be wrote* by me.' Sermon eleven included a bit more and sermon twelve is remarkable in its simple, easy-to-remember outline based on the wording of the well-known verse. Those who have examined Whitefield's preaching style mention that many times he would preach on one verse, after putting it in context.[7] These fifteen sermons are typical of that style. Newton included Whitefield's expansion of each of the points and then how he applied them to his audience. Whitefield had a unique application and challenge to the listeners. Newton commented on this pattern in sermon twelve. 'He divided his application *as usual* so that everyone had something [emphasis added].' Whitefield was quite direct and focused in his application. In sermon eleven, he spoke to each of the three groups of listeners: those who were followers of Jesus, those who were backsliders, and those who were not followers of Jesus. Or as Newton succinctly summarises of sermon fifteen, 'He applyed* these things to both saints and

---

7. Lee Gatiss, ed., *The Sermons of George Whitefield* (Wheaton, Ill., 2012), 1:22.

sinners.' And he always preached for a response. As in sermon three to the 5,000 gathered, the great evangelist gave 'an offer and pressing invitation to the gospel.'

At the end of many sermon entries, Newton recorded how he had been affected. Of sermon ten, he writes, 'cheared* my poor cold heart. I was led to see that I do through grace feed upon Christ in my heart by faith with thanksgiving, that the Lord has brought me willingly to Christ and enabled me to believe on him; and that in consequence thereof, my hunger and thirst after this world and its vanities are abated. I find something of a sweet satisfaction where before there was a void and emptiness.' Of sermon twelve, he wrote, 'Surely, the Lord opened my heart; at this time the tears run down my eyes with joy, that I could understand and through grace have experienced something of these divine things.' This sermon touched him emotionally. But it is important to note that his tears of joy were the result of the Lord opening his heart to a fresh understanding of biblical truth. In many ways Newton's notes and his reflections show that his diary was in the true sense a spiritual journal. His diary notations were not in any way like Gurney's transcriptions of Whitefield's sermons, mentioned earlier. Instead Newton's notations were a dynamic combination of what he heard and how he processed it and applied it personally.

Later, after Whitefield travelled on from Liverpool, Newton could turn to his published sermons. For example, the Sunday following his second rejection to ordination, he read Whitefield's sermon about Enoch

'Walking with God' (Gen. 5:34).[8] By this time, Newton was in the habit of periodically having a few friends to his home on Sunday evenings and called them his 'congregation.' That night he read that sermon to his guests and commented afterwards, 'had a pleasant time.'[9] When they had gone home, he continued to meditate on that passage about Enoch, whom Whitefield described as 'a flaming preacher.' Whitefield, in typical fashion, applied the text to his audience and at the closing challenged the pastors who were in the congregation. He declared that preachers have 'the honour' of being public 'ambassadors of Christ and stewards of the mysteries of Christ.' He challenged them, as well as himself, to be faithful like Enoch. 'Does he not yet speak to us, to quicken our zeal and make us more active in the service of our glorious and ever-blessed Master?'[10] Newton was thankful that God had blessed his efforts thus far. 'Unworthy as I am, the Lord has made me useful to some.' No doubt he was thinking of his many one-on-one conversations, as well as the meetings of the society and at his home. Responding to Whitefield's challenge, he now prayed for 'more zeal and prudence.' But he longed for a larger sphere of ministry and pondered the two ordination rejections. 'I would hope he has not laid me aside.'[11] In response, he chose to follow the faithful example of Enoch and persevere.

---

8. Gatiss, *Sermons of George Whitefield*, 1:64-81.

9. Diary [2], 25 Feb. 1759.

10. Gatiss, *Sermons of George Whitefield*, 1:81.

11. Diary [2], 25 Feb. 1759.

His Leading the Communion Service

Whitefield's large communion service 8 June 1755 (sermon three) at the Tabernacle overwhelmed Newton. Two things in particular resonated with his spirit and reinforced what would be Newton's trademarks for the rest of his life.

The Power of Hymn Singing

He found the hymn singing in the communion service quite stirring. It was not only the singing in the service that impressed him, but it was how Whitefield integrated it into the free flowing liturgy. What he experienced that day reinforced in his mind the value of hymn singing. 'He made many little intervals for singing hymns—I believe nearly 20 times in all.' Newton gave more details to Polly. 'Every ten minutes or oftener we stopped and sung part of a hymn, I suppose 20 different times in all or more.'[12] In his study of Newton's preaching and hymnody, Wesleyan historian Donald Demaray noticed this comment and that Whitefield published a hymnbook (1753) for his Tabernacle. But Demaray overstates it when he says, 'It was Whitefield more than any other who was ultimately responsible for Newton's use of hymns at Olney.'[13] Newton had sung Isaac Watts' hymns as a child, so he was quite aware of hymn singing, in contrast to singing just psalms, as was the common

---

12. Newton to Polly, (no date, but contents place it June 10 or 11, 1755), MS 2935 (f. 218) at Lambeth Palace. See also Cecil/Rouse, *Newton*, 90, 91.

13. Demaray, *The Innovation of John Newton*, 201.

practice in the Established Church.[14] Certainly singing was a vital part of the Evangelical Revival. And one cannot overlook the great hymn-writer Charles Wesley and that his brother John published a congregational hymnbook a few months after Whitefield.[15] But it certainly can be said that Newton was inspired by the singing, and the way in which Whitefield integrated it into his communion service. No doubt it had also moved him when he joined in singing from Whitefield's hymnbook at the Tabernacle, even when Whitefield was away. Consequently, it is not surprising that nine years later in Olney, Newton made hymn-singing a key component of his services and meetings. As stated earlier, his desire to have hymns that reinforced his sermons resulted in many times composing them himself. Following Whitefield's example, he published a hymn book (*Olney Hymns*, 1779) for his congregation's benefit. Though unlike Whitefield's, all were by Newton and Cowper.[16]

The Beauty of the Unity of Believers
Newton was profoundly moved by Whitefield's emphasis on the unity of believers, rather than on denominations or secondary doctrines. He was

---

14. Rouse/Cecil, *Newton*, 15.

15. Tyerman, *Whitefield*, 2:294, 295. Tyerman points out that soon after in that year, Wesley published a hymnbook for his own congregation.

16. See Hindmarsh, *Newton*, 264, for Newton's further comments about the blessing of hymn singing, especially those by Watts *Hymns and Spiritual Songs* (1707). Also see 257-288 on Newton's hymnody.

truly stirred when sitting with over a thousand believers 'of different persuasions.' But what impressed him particularly was that they 'all agreed in the *great essentials* of the gospel, and in *mutual charity* worshipping the Lord with *one heart and soul* [emphasis added].' Similarly he reported to Polly, that they 'met together with one heart and soul, though of different forms and persuasions [being] church folks [Established Church], Baptists, Presbyterians, etc.' who all 'agreed in the grand fundamentals of our faith.' Further these worshippers had lives that were consistent with their faith and they 'bore testimony of a suitable practice.'[17] Continuing, he exclaimed, 'never before had I such an idea and foretaste of the business of heaven.' Whitefield's last will and testament, written a few months before he died, clearly expresses his final wish for unity. 'Grace be with all them, of whatever denomination, that love our Lord Jesus, our common Lord, in sincerity.'[18] Similarly, Newton said, 'I love his people of all names and of all ranks. I long for their prosperity and am glad of every opportunity to contribute my mite thereto.'[19]

Through Whitefield's Personal Ministry

In Conversation
In contrast to his London experience, in Liverpool Newton had the privilege of spending much time

---

17. Newton to Polly, n.d. MS 2935 (f. 218) at Lambeth Palace.

18. Quoted in Tyerman, *Whitefield*, 2:609, 610.

19. Diary [2], 18 Jan. 1766.

with Whitefield during his visit to the town. He sat
or walked with him at least seven times. He excitedly
shared the details with Polly. 'I went to see him and
conversed with him [for two hours] the next morning,
when he invited me to supper. I went home with him
from the preaching, and stayed till ten o'clock.' With
pleasure, he exclaimed, 'So now we are *very great*,'[20]
which meant in that day 'close, on intimate terms and
much acquainted.' In all they ate together five times.
'I ... supped with him three times and dined with him
once at Mr. F's, and on Sunday, he dined with me.'[21]
It is important to observe that Newton's talks with
Whitefield were not interviews. They were much
deeper than that! For example, he described the two-
hour session as 'close conversation' that brought him
'great comfort and satisfaction.' Newton was moved
to apply these to his life. For example that week Newton fulfilled the pledge he had made in London that
he would not be hesitant to identify with Methodists
like Whitefield. This time, he invited his prejudiced
landlady to hear Whitefield and on the second day she
did go. Afterward, when she asked Newton to invite
Whitefield for dinner, Newton (with her approval) invited five more friends to join them. Newton was publicly so much with him that his friends dubbed him
'young Whitefield.' But it no longer mattered to him;
in fact he called it 'an honour.' The previous year in St.
Kitts, Captain Clunie had challenged Newton to make
his faith more public. He was now increasingly willing

---

20. *Letters to a Wife*, 12 September 1755 in *Works* 5: 502, 503.

21. *Letters to a Wife*, 26 September 1755 in *Works* 5: 503.

to do that. But this was not some kind of hero worship. He was publicly identifying with the faith and doctrine Whitefield proclaimed.

Whitefield's conversations were sources of much personal encouragement to Newton. When Newton was setting out for a less-than-impressive place of ministry in Warwick, he purposefully 'scratch'd up pretty early' to hear Whitefield preach. Immediately after the sermon, this famous and busy pastor-evangelist invited Newton for breakfast. That, in itself made Newton's early rising worth it. But it was the conversation that Newton so savoured; so much so, he wished that Polly had been there to sit in on it. It was very encouraging for him that Whitefield was '*greatly* pleas'd [emphasis added]' with his plan to go for a trial period at the Warwick chapel, when others, including some of his in-laws were not in favour of it. It was also reassuring to have Whitefield affirm his yearning 'to engage in the good work [in this case meaning pastoral ministry] some way or other ... and not remain silent.'[22] Even though in the end Newton turned down the permanent call, at least Newton had this revered evangelist affirm the direction he was taking.

Prior to this, when Whitefield had been in Liverpool, he gave Newton some helpful advice that would have major impact on Newton's time in that town. As stated earlier, when Newton first went there to serve as Tide Surveyor, he began to attend John Johnson's Baptist church. He especially valued Johnson's dynamic preaching that has recently been described as

---

22. Quoted in Martin, *Newton*, 191 and transcription by Rouse.

'solemn and majestic.'[23] However, Whitefield recommended the other Baptist pastor John Oulton whom he described as 'an excellent humble man.'[24] Whitefield's words 'excellent humble' may be a clue to the concern he had. In contrast, Johnson has been described as 'with an originality of mind,' and 'unafraid of controversy,' who 'attacked Anglicans, Methodists, and other Baptists in print.'[25]

In part, Johnson's conflicts were caused by his theological speculations that led him to some odd (and in some cases, unorthodox) conclusions. These had split Byrom Street Baptist in about 1747/8 when he was the pastor. One Baptist historian admits that Johnson was 'talented' but describes parts of his theology as 'bizarre.'[26] His critics accused him of unorthodox views of the Trinity (a charge he denied). As a result of his publications, as well as his preaching tours, a few churches (especially in the north) followed him in forming a separate small Baptist association (c.1757), often called Johnsonian Baptists. Because of their emphasis on purity of truth they would not fellowship with any Baptist churches outside their small association.[27]

Certainly, if Newton heard only Johnson, he was at risk of being negatively influenced by him. Nineteen

23. Copson, 'Johnson, John (1705/6-1791),' ODNB.

24. Diary [1], 21 Sept. 1755.

25. Copson, 'Johnson, John (1705/6-1791),' ODNB.

26. Brown, Eighteenth Century Baptists, 86.

27. Unless indicated otherwise, in this paragraph I am following R. Dawbarn, 'The Johnsonian Baptists', Transactions of the Baptist Historical Society, 3 (1912–13): 54–61 and S. L. Copson, 'Johnson, John (1705/6–1791)', ODNB. For list of ten of their distinct doctrines see Dawbarn, 59, 60.

years later, that happened temporarily to the brilliant twenty-one-year old Andrew Fuller (1853-1813) who later became one of the great Baptist theologians. Fuller confessed how Johnson's publications caused him to be 'much perplexed.' Fuller mentions in particular there were two things that Johnson pleaded: 'That God did not and could not decree to permit evil, without being the author of it – and that he would have glorified his elect, though sin had never intervened.' Looking back on this, Fuller described these speculations as, in the words of Bunyan, 'nuts which spoil the children's teeth.' Of these thoughts, Fuller went on to say, 'I have considered an attachment to them as resembling the chewing of certain narcotics, of which, though they are generally disagreeable at first, yet, by a little use of them, some persons become so fond, as to prefer them to their bread.'[28]

Fortunately, despite attending both Baptist churches on many Sundays, Newton shows discernment about Johnson's extremes. For example, in one sermon, Newton noted that Johnson 'laboured much ... to shew* that assurance when once obtained can upon no case or supposition be lost or withdrawn.' This was one of the tenets of Johnsonian Baptists.[29] Of this, Newton responded, 'I cannot agree with him herein.' Further, Newton said this belief was not useful because it caused people to focus on the strength of

---

28. John Ryland (jr.), ed., *The Work of Faith, the Labour of Love and the Patience of Hope: Illustrated in the Life and Death of Rev. Andrew Fuller* (2 edn., London, 1818), 34.

29. Johnsonian Baptists taught that 'every believer knows he is a child of God and that therefore doubt is inconsistent with such assurance' (Dawburn, 'Johnsonian Baptists,' 59, 60).

their own attainments and not on the Lord's grace.[30] In another sermon, Johnson endeavoured 'to explain and accommodate the image of Nebuchadnezzar's dream' to prophetic details. Newton admitted that Johnson 'took occasion to introduce many useful observations,' but Newton complained, 'the bulk of his discourse was rather curious, if not strained.'[31] Gradually, Newton attended Johnson's church less and less, and the final diary record of his being there was in mid-August 1758, when he heard a guest preacher. That sermon had many 'sound truths' but Newton thought it was for him 'cold and heavy.' Though Newton admitted the fault was partly his own, he also believed listeners are much influenced by the 'instruments and manner of preaching.'[32]

Providentially for Newton, Oulton's ministry served as a balance to Johnson's. Newton's diary shows that he had many one-on-one conversations with Oulton, whereas he had few with Johnson. For example in March 1759 when in the midst of dealing with rejections from the Established Church, Newton records, 'had Mr. Oulton as usual in the afternoon with Mr. Wilson. Had some spiritual conversation.'[33] A few months later, 'Mr. Oulton joined in the [Monday] afternoon, we had much conversation.'[34] When Newton was trying to decide whether or not to accept

---

30. Diary [2], 19 Dec. 1756.

31. Diary [2], 2 Oct. 1757.

32. Diary [2], Sunday 13 Aug. 1758.

33. Diary [2], Monday 5 March 1759.

34. Diary [2], 3 Sept. 1759.

the invitation for an interim try-out at Warwick, he records, 'Mr Oulton with me and no other company.'[35]

Further, in contrast to Johnson, Oulton was not an isolationist. Newton was pleased to notice this when he first met him and visited one of his parishioners. 'They seem to enjoy a catholic free spirit and are not bound up within the limits of a party as some here and too many everywhere are.'[36] Therefore, Oulton provided a link to the Revival that was happening in other parts of England. For example, the next year Newton was at Oulton's for tea when a 'brother from the country' shared the exciting update of the revival that 'there are not less than twenty gospel ministers in the Church of England in and about Bristol and who hold a monthly meeting there.'[37] This was wonderful news to them. Still thinking of this a week later, and just before leaving to attend church that morning, Newton lifted up his concerns to God. 'I particularly prayed for this town of Liverpool, in which I reside, that, if it please* the Lord, we may partake of that great enlightening which is breaking forth in different places on the Church of England side.'[38] That tea-time conversation was one of a series of events that reinforced Newton's concern for renewal in the Established Church and led to his own longing to serve the Church.

Newton gradually saw the limitations of Johnson's preaching. For example, on one Sunday he heard Oulton twice and Johnson once. Oulton's two

---

35. Diary [2], 2 Jan. 1760.
36. Diary [1], 22 Sept. 1755.
37. Diary [1], 18 March 1756.
38. Diary [1], 28 March 1756.

sermons touched his heart and he said, 'through grace I was helped to apply ... [the examples] all to myself.' Whereas, of the evening sermon, Newton said Johnson delivered 'many good things' but lamented, 'in his accustomed manner no inference, application or distinction of his hearers.'[39] Six months earlier, when he first heard Oulton, he observed that though Oulton was not as gifted as Johnson at preaching doctrine, he dealt more in application which Newton said, 'I have always found the most useful to me.'[40] This is what he admired in Whitefield, and now he found it also in the less dramatic Oulton.

In Correspondence

Whitefield is known today for his outstanding preaching, but he was also a conscientious letter writer. For example, 'After a full day of preaching, exhorting, and counselling, Whitefield would often stay up past midnight answering his correspondents and addressing their spiritual needs.'[41] As seen in his correspondence with Newton, Whitefield was quick to respond to his letter. His letter (8 Aug. 1765) to Newton was especially heartening. Whitefield had just arrived back from his two-year mission to America, was exhausted, and felt like a 'shattered bark... scarce worth docking anymore.' Therefore, it is significant that he would immediately answer Newton's letter the day it came. This reveals how highly Whitefield valued Newton, who had by this time pastored in Olney for a year. By

---

39. Diary [1], 28 March 1756.

40. Diary [1], 21 Sept. 1755.

41. Hindmarsh, *The Evangelical Conversion Narrative*, 74. See also Dallimore, *Whitefield*, 2:284.

the content of the letter, it appears that this was the first time Whitefield heard about Newton's move to Olney. The news 'gladdened' Whitefield's heart. In his letter Whitefield praises God for not only calling Newton into pastoral ministry but also calling him to Olney. In many ways, this was a kind of an Elijah blessing over this newly ordained Elisha. Further, Whitefield pledged to pray for Newton and his 'dear flock.' In closing, Whitefield promised to visit Olney when he recovered, 'to join my testimony *with yours* in Olney pulpit, that God is love [emphasis added].' Here the great evangelist treated Newton, the new pastor, as a peer *with* whom he would stand.

WHITEFIELD'S INDIRECT IMPACT ON NEWTON
It is important to notice that Whitefield influenced New-ton indirectly through active supporters of Whitefield's ministry. In London, it began with Samuel Hayward and Samuel Brewer who mentored him and introduced Newton to Whitefield. The deep affection Brewer had for Whitefield began, as we have seen, when Brewer was a student and continued throughout Whitefield's life. This is seen in Brewer's brief note to him a week before Whitefield preached his farewell sermon; before setting sail for what would be his final mission to America.[42]

Dear Sir,

I am so poorly with my cold that I am deprived of the great pleasure of dineing* with you today at Dear Mr. [name blocked out] and of being at the Tabernacle this evening. But I purpose God willing to be Tottenham

---

42. The farewell sermon was 30 Aug. 1769 and he embarked for America in late September (Kidd, *Whitefield*, 246, 247).

Court tomorrow at half after 12 to spend one half hour with you.

I cannot tell you how [much] I love you and what sense I have of all the tokens of your Brotherly kindness to me. My heart feels a pain beyond description [that] you are going to leave us, but I believe you go because you think tis your duty, and I know I shall join thousands in praying that the God of Israel may be your protector and that in all places, by land and sea, you may enjoy the Lord's presence and blessing.

I hope we shall meet again on earth, but above all I pray we may meet in glory to sing eternally the Song of Moses to the Lamb.

I am my Dear Bro[r]
Yours Sincerely & affectionately
S. Brewer[43]

Gillies informs us that upon Whitefield's death, Brewer was one of the many pastors who preached a memorial sermon. Though 'which his modesty would not permit him to print.'[44]

Other Whitefield supporters included John Berridge, Andrew Gifford, Martin Madan, William Romaine, and Henry Venn whom Newton connected with along his journey to ordination and who were his pastoral friends afterwards. There was also William Grimshaw who, though selected by John Wesley to be his successor,

---

43. Brewer to Whitefield, 23 Aug. 1769, (MS in Bridwell Library, Special Collections, Perkins School of Theology, SMU, TX.

44. Gillies, *Whitefield*, 245. Rouse indicates he preached from Ps. 37:37, 'Mark the perfect man, and behold the upright: for the end of that man is peace' (Cecil/Rouse, *Newton*, 338).

also had collegial connections with Whitefield and invited him to join in services with him. In viewing this
list, one quickly recognises that this is the who's who of
the Evangelical Revival and reveals Newton's large circle
of pastoral friends. Of course, the list also includes John
and Charles Wesley, though Newton joined Whitefield's
ranks. It is quite amazing that in the providence of God,
Newton would have contact with so many even before
his ordination. It also speaks well of Newton's discernment that he sought out the counsel of mature pastors in
the Evangelical Revival.

His road to ordination and coming to Olney was, hu-
manly speaking, the result of three of Whitefield's circle.
First was John Fawcett who had been converted under
Whitefield and who asked Newton to write down the details of his life. The second was Thomas Haweis who asked
Newton to expand the letters and published them as *An
Authentic Narrative*. At that time Haweis had an interesting,
though not well-known connection with Whitefield. In
1763, Whitefield who was commissioned to find a suitable
minister for St. Paul's Episcopal Church in Philadelphia,
pressed Haweis to accept it. Though he declined.[45] Previously, for the same position Whitefield had without success sought Romaine, another friend of Newton's.[46] The
third was Lord Dartmouth who used his influence to overcome Newton's major hurdle to ordination. Because he
doggedly pressed the hierarchy of the Established Church,

---

45. A. Skevington Wood, *Thomas Haweis* (1734-1820 (London, 1957),
103.

46. Tim Shenton, *The Life and Times of William Romaine* (Darlington,
2004), 195; A. Skevington Wood, *Thomas Haweis*, 103.

they somewhat reluctantly agreed to ordain Newton. The fact, that in the end his ordination could be processed in a matter of a few weeks, shows that their previous excuses were unfounded and indeed a sham. Or to use Wesley's terms, a 'farce' and 'so poor an evasion!'[47]

As we have seen, Whitefield's ministry had positively impacted the town of Olney before Newton arrived. Consequently, Olney was more receptive to his ministry. It made Newton's first years of ministry in his first church so much easier and he acknowledged his indebtedness to Whitefield. In addition, financial help came from Whitefield supporters. Dartmouth not only paid for Newton's 'living' at the church of St. Peter and St. Paul in Olney but renovated the vicarage and provided a large room in the Great House for Newton's expanding ministry needs. John Thornton used his wealth to provide Newton with generous subsidy (for hospitality and local benevolence) for his sixteen-year ministry in Olney. Afterwards, he was the one who made it possible for Newton to move to St. Mary Woolnoth, London. This move brought Newton into a new sphere of influence in the centre of London.

---

47. 20 March 1760 in Ward and Heitzenrater, *Works of John Wesley*, 21: 248.

8

Comparisons between Whitefield and Newton

Both Disliked Denominational and Doctrinal Conflict
Whitefield, though he boldly castigated unconverted and lukewarm Established Church clergy, especially in his younger years, was not one to stir up controversy among fellow believers. Yes it is true that Whitefield and Wesley had their doctrinal differences and these eventually resulted in forming two streams of Methodism (Calvinistic Methodist and Wesleyan Methodist). But this was not what Whitefield wanted. In Liverpool, Newton remembered that Whitefield had said he was 'cautious of introducing a division amongst the Methodists.' Wesley commented on this quality, when Whitefield visited him, 31 January 1766. 'Mr. Whitefield called upon me. He breathes nothing but peace and love. Bigotry cannot stand before him, but hides its head wherever he comes.'[1] Newton saw this modelled in Whitefield and sought to be the same. He transparently acknowledged in his preface that some hymns in his hymnbook had Calvinistic themes. 'I am a friend of peace; and being convinced that no one can profitably understand the great truths and doctrines of the Gospel any farther than he

---

1. Wesley diary quoted in Tyerman, *Whitefield*, 2:492.

is taught of God I have not a wish to obtrude [impose] my own tenants upon others, in a way of controversy; yet I do not think myself bound to conceal them.'[2] Wesley saw this quality in Newton too, and said to him, 'You appear to be designed by God to be a healer of breaches, a reconciler of honest but prejudiced men, and a uniter (happy work!) of the children of God that are needlessly divided from each other.'[3] Newton had seen the damage caused by fighting over secondary doctrines. He later said, 'To draw those who are engaged in one cause into contest about words and phrases is an old device of the enemy .... And I have met with an expression, which though not very delicately expressed, stands in my mind as a maxim, confirmed by the experience of ages, *Pruritus disputandi scabies ecclesiae* [meaning basically, an itch for disputing is the infection of the church].'[4]

This does not mean that Newton thought doctrine was unimportant. This is clearly seen in his letter to Whitefield (2 Jan. 1756) in which he agonised over the fact that in Liverpool 'the tenets of the Arians and Socinians are not only held, but propagated with the most pernicious address; the satisfaction and divinity of the blessed Jesus slighted and degraded.' That is why he pled for preachers who have 'skill to divide the word of truth in a lively, affecting manner' and who 'dwell upon the great essentials of the gospel in the first place, to inform the people of the truths in which all renewed Christians agree, before they puzzle them with the points on which we differ.'[5]

---

2. Preface in *Olney Hymns* in *Works*, 3:303.

3. Quoted in Hindmarsh, *Newton*, 328.

4. Quoted in Gordon, *Wise Counsel*, 258.

5. Newton to Whitefield, 2 January 1756, MS 2935 (ff. 232, 233) at Lambeth Palace.

It is interesting to see that Newton had specific goals when he moved to St. Mary Woolnoth in downtown London. 'My congregations are made up from all parts and from all parties. I trust I am enabled to speak plainly and faithfully, but you know I am a friend of peace. I declare my sentiments of the truth, but do not offer to force them down people's throats. So far as I can judge, my call in this city, besides preaching the salvation of God to sinners is twofold. 1. To inculcate peace and love among those who are upon the one foundation, though in some points they are not all of one mind. 2. To insist much upon the life of God in the soul, and to show that the power of religion is something different from attachment to systems or modes or forms.'[6] In this Newton largely succeeded. He was able to report that 'Church folks and Dissenters of different names – Methodists from Tabernacle [and] from Foundery, Moravians, and if I mistake not sometimes Quakers, gather round me and sit as quiet as many lambs.'[7]

Both Had a Large Vision

Whitefield modelled a huge vision. He crossed the ocean thirteen times, and while in the colonies traversed up and down the east coast. In England he preached in the big cities and even little out-of-way poor towns like Olney and made many tours to Scotland. In contrast, Newton did not travel out of England but he did have a vision beyond himself. It is revealing that within a few months of settling into a very good occupation and into life with Polly in their new home in Liverpool, his heart

---

6. Newton to Ryland, 7 Sept. 1780 in Gordon, *Wise Counsel*, 144.

7. Gordon, *Wise Counsel*, 144.

was beginning to break. This pain was not for himself, or his circle of friends, but for the whole town. He movingly expressed this in his letter (2 Jan. 1756) to Whitefield. 'Here are more than forty thousand people, who in matters of religion hardly know their right hand from their left.' And he is much 'pained and ashamed' with the little group at the local Methodist Meeting House, which he attended periodically, that was divided and inward thinking. 'Shall 30 or 40 such, keep out an opportunity of declaring the grace of God to *thousands*? I hope not!' So he pled for Whitefield, or his preachers, even Wesley (whom he had heard about, but not heard personally) to come. '*Come over hither and help us...* I beg dear sir, you will bear us in mind, perhaps Providence may show you a way of assisting us.'

When Newton became a pastor in Olney, his immediate focus was on his flock, but quickly it stretched out further. Soon he was visiting and preaching in the nearby counties and travelling further afield preaching in parishes of his evangelical clergy friends.[8] His move to St. Mary Woolnoth, in a less residential area of London, meant that he had more time to minister beyond his local church. 'On Sunday afternoons I frequently preach in other Churches up and down the city. And frequently in the course of the week speak to a select few in private houses. So that I need not grow rusty for want of employment.'[9] In addition, through correspondence he kept abreast of what was happening in England, Scotland, and the American colonies. Through his personal letters he provided

---

8. See map in Hindmarsh, *Newton*, 210.

9. Quoted in Gordon, *Wise Counsel*, 144.

pastoral counsel to most areas of the English speaking world. He was vitally interested in missions therefore was influential in having chaplains sent to India and Australia, and corresponded with them afterwards.[10] He was also instrumental in the forming of the *Church Missionary Society*, and advocating for other mission agencies. [11]

Both Were Loyal to the Established Church

Whitefield modelled how one could remain loyal to the Established Church and its doctrines, and be a faithful evangelical. In reviewing the life of Whitefield, Dallimore says, 'His loyalty remained basically with the Church of England.'[12] Whitefield said this in his preface to his hymn-book (c.1755). 'As for those against any offices or set form at all, I shall only say, "Let not him who useth a form judge him who useth it not; and let not him who useth it not despise him who doth use it." I profess myself to be a minister of the Established Church, and never yet renounced her articles, homilies or liturgy.'[13] When Newton was seeking to become a pastor, he found it difficult to choose a denomination. He was sought by Congregationalists, Presbyterians, and for a time by John Wesley. He had issues with some statements in the Established

---

10. Gordon, *Wise Counsel*, 202, 203, 206.

11. Ibid., 361, 365, 366.

12. Dallimore, *Whitefield* (1990), 165. See also Lee Gatiss, 'George Whitefield: The Anglican Evangelist,' *The Southern Baptist Journal of Theology* (Summer 2014): 71-81. He describes Whitefield's itinerant ministry as that of an 'Anglican cavalryman' and the evangelical Anglican clergy settled in one location, such as James Hervey, William Romaine and Augustus Toplady, as 'regular guardsmen.'

13. Tyerman, *Whitefield*, 2:345.

Church *Book of Common Prayer* (in the baptism and burial sections) but Crooke explained how he could follow the *Book* and still do so in keeping with his conscience.[14] Other Established clergy encouraged him, as did Whitefield.

Years later, after becoming a pastor, some Dissenters were critical of him remaining in the Established Church. Therefore, he wrote his defence called *Apologia* (1784).[15] In this he listed his reasons for continuing to serve in the Established Church. The Church gave him freedom to do his ministry, without the restraints he had seen in many chapels and meeting-houses. Serving in the Church gave him greater possibility of reaching others for Christ because he believed the vast majority of people were part of the Established Church who would never enter a chapel. God had led him into the Established Church. It is true, he admitted, that the hierarchy had opposed his entry but this taught him humility and patience. In the end, he had the assurance that 'I was following the call and doing the will of God ... as if an angel had been sent to tell me so.'[16] He admitted the liturgy was not perfect. 'As to our liturgy, I am far from thinking it incapable of amendment; though, when I consider the temper and spirit of the present times, I dare not wish that the improvement of it should be attempted, lest the intended remedy might prove worse than the disease.'[17] In the end he thought

14. Aitken, *Newton*, 152. See also Hindmarsh, *Newton*, 87, 88 in which he explains that Newton was opposed to any statements in the prayer book that imply baptismal regeneration or that an unconverted person had 'a sure and certain hope of the Resurrection.'

15. *Works* 5:1-58.

16. Quoted in Aitken, *Newton*, 285.

17. *Works* 5:10.

the 'general strain' of the present liturgy was 'scriptural, evangelical and experimental.'[18] He also responded to the Dissenters who complained about Established clergy following written prayers in official services. 'Many who profess to pray extempore, that is, without either a printed or written form, go so much in a beaten path, that they who hear them frequently can tell, with tolerable certainty, how they will begin, when they are about in the middle, and when they are drawing towards the close of their prayer.'[19]

Both Became Celebrities in Their Own Right

From the very beginning, people were drawn to see and hear Whitefield. At twenty-one, when he preached his first sermon in his home church in Gloucester (June 1736), he noted that 'curiosity drew a large congregation together.'[20] By the end of 1737, as a result of Whitefield's extensive preaching in London and just before he sailed to America, Mark Noll concludes that 'he had become London's best known celebrity.'[21] The same thing happened in America. All kinds of people were drawn to hear him. Many were serious, some came to scoff, and others were just there to see this famous preacher. For example, in Philadelphia, 1739, 'an estimated audience of six thousand *curious* onlookers – nearly half of Philadelphia's urban population (emphasis added)' gathered to hear him.[22] As a travelling evangelist

---

18. *Works* 5:10.

19. *Works* 5:11, 12.

20. Mahaffey, *The Accidental Revolutionary*, 15.

21. Noll, *The Rise of Evangelicalism*, 89.

22. Stout, *Divine Dramatist*, 90.

in America he used advance newspaper notices and letters to announce his coming. In addition, he contracted Benjamin Franklin, the editor of the Pennsylvania Gazette and an admirer of Whitefield, to publish his journals.[23] Consequently, Whitefield became the 'best-known person in eighteenth-century America.'[24]

When Newton came to Olney in 1764, he was unknown to most people. But when his autobiography, *An Authentic Narrative*, was published a few months later, that quickly began to change. Newton's identity was not mentioned, but soon word spread that it was John Newton, the curate in Olney. Consequently he became a celebrity in the town and nearby villages. The former slave-ship captain was now a pastor. Newton saw this popularity as a positive thing. 'I have reason to hope that the publication of my letters will give some additional weight to my ministry here. The people stare at me since reading them, as well they may. I am indeed a wonder to many – a wonder to myself. Especially I wonder that I wonder no more.'[25] He reported to his friend Clunie that 'it is pleasing to see people flocking from all quarters.'[26] Drawn by Newton's fame, many travelled from outside the parish boundaries, from nearby Northamptonshire and Bedfordshire and occasionally from London.[27] Consequently, within a year of coming to Olney, a gallery in the sanctuary had to be built to handle the increasing attendance.

---

23. Stout, *Divine Dramatist*, 102.

24. On book jacket of Mahaffey, *The Accidental Revolutionary*.

25. Newton to Clunie, 11 Dec. 1764, Newton (Clunie), 62.

26. Newton to Clunie, 4 Aug. 1765, Newton (Clunie), 83.

27. Aitken, *Newton*, 190.

In 1780, when Newton moved to London, he was already well-known in the evangelical world through his life story (*An Authentic Narrative*) and his *Olney Hymns* (1779). Within a few months, he noticed that in the morning service the church was 'rather large' and the evening 'full.'[28] Though, this positive response did not sit well with everyone. Some of his parishioners complained to the church leadership that when they arrived at church their seats were either taken, or they could not get to them because of the crowd in the aisles. To resolve this, one of the churchwardens came to him with, what he thought was, a simple solution. Newton, no doubt chuckled when he shared it with Polly. 'He proposed with many apologies my letting another clergyman preach now and then for me; hinted it should be no expense to me, and thought that if it was uncertain whether I preached or no, the people would not throng the church so much.' Newton responded that he could do nothing about it once the church doors were opened, but did agree to give announcement to the parishioners 'to dispose them to be good-humoured* to strangers.' [29] 'People wanted to see this curious ... man who had led such a remarkably adventurous life in his seafaring days ... the novelty of this man never wore off.'[30] But it was more than his adventurous past. It was that despite his wretched life, God had reached down and saved this 'African blasphemer,' as Newton often referred to himself. Certainly, Newton never got over God's amazing grace that had rescued him and set him eventually on a path into pastoral ministry.

28. Quoted in Gordon, *Wise Counsel*, 144.

29. Quoted in Bull, *Newton*, 247.

30. Demaray, *Newton*, 183.

Both Were Adept at Using Visual Language and Metaphors

'Whitefield's field preaching relied heavily on imagination and dramatisation.'[31] Kidd notes that 'often when retelling Bible stories, Whitefield set scenes with the thoughts, feelings, and appearance of characters.'[32] Hence he often preached on biblical stories and images and did so in such a way that would captivate the massive crowds. Many of Whitefield's sermons that Newton recorded were this kind. These include sermons (4) thirst; (5) prison; (7) re-commissioning of Peter; (8) storms; (10) bread, hunger, thirst; (11) Jesus the way; (12) Christ knocking at door, Lazarus; (13) sleeping, Peter's denial, prodigal son; and (15) clothing. One can see how Whitefield, with his unique expressive skills, could draw the crowd into these stories in such a way that they were no longer detached listeners but engaged participants. Seymour says that Whitefield's 'metaphors were drawn from sources easily understood by his hearers, and frequently from the circumstances of the moment.'[33]

Newton did not have Whitefield's flair for the dramatic in his sermons, but he did have a creative imagination and the ability to use striking images or easy-to-remember metaphors in his writing. This is seen in his most famous hymn, *Amazing Grace*, where he uses images of lost and found; blind and see; dangers, toils and snares; and shield. This ability is especially true of his personal

---

31. Stout, *Divine Dramatist*, 93.

32. Kidd, *Whitefield*, 155. He also states that Whitefield would introduce a biblical event with the words 'methinks I see' and then describe what the person or people in the story saw or felt.

33. Seymour, *The Life and Times of Selina*, 1:91.

letters. For example, to a young married pastor experiencing deep stress, he wrote. 'Trials, my dear friend, of one kind or other, to prove, exercise and manifest our faith, patience and grace, are as necessary to us, as weights are to a [grandfather] clock; if they were not we should [not] have them. For the Lord does not grieve us for his own pleasure, but for our profit.'[34] So much truth is packed in this image of weights in a clock and that difficulties are not random or out-of-control events but overseen by a caring God, who does not cause grief because he enjoys it, but for our profit. Having spent many years on the sea, he often used nautical images. To the same pastor, he gave this advice. 'And the tongue of the truly learned, that can speak a word in season to them that are weary, is not acquired, like Greek and Latin, by reading great books; but by self-knowledge and soul exercises. To learn navigation by the fire-side, will never make a man an expert mariner. He must do his business in great waters. And practice will bring him into many situations, of which his general theory could give him no conception.'[35]

DIFFERENCES BETWEEN WHITEFIELD AND NEWTON

It is important to note that Newton did not try to be a copy of Whitefield. The following two examples show that Newton was not a carbon copy of Whitefield.

Their Marriages

At the risk of being simplistic, a railway metaphor comes to mind. John Wesley's marriage was a train wreck (Wesleyan historian, Henry Rack called it a 'disaster'

---

34. Quoted in Gordon, *Wise Counsel*, 177.

35. Quoted in Gordon, *Wise Counsel*, 243.

and 'catastrophe'[36]); Whitefield's was a freight train (satisfactory but functional); and Newton's was a scenic passenger train (enjoyable and relational). Even Dallimore, who revered Whitefield, is forced to admit that Whitefield's marriage was at best 'tolerably happy.'[37] Elizabeth was supportive of her husband's ministry and went with him on one mission to America. But other times they were separated for long periods and it appears that often his mission took precedence over their marriage.[38] In contrast, when Lord Dartmouth asked Newton to accept the presidency of the proposed college in Georgia, Newton first considered his Polly and his marriage, and then declined the offer. Further, his devotion to her was so strong that after she died in 1790 he edited his long correspondence and published it as *Letters to a Wife* (1793). The deep affection he expressed in these letters was quite remarkable for that day (especially for clergy). Whitefield's marriage gradually became a disappointment for both George and Elizabeth.[39] In contrast the relationship between John and Polly grew stronger with age. In a letter to Polly, Newton expressed his marriage this way, 'My love has been growing from the day of marriage [twenty-four years prior] and still it is in a growing state. It was once as an acorn, but it has now a deep root, and

---

36. Henry D. Rack, *Reasonable Enthusiast: John Wesley and the Rise of Methodism* (3rd ed., London, 2002), 257. For details, see Rack, 257-269, and Richard P. Heitzenrater, *The Elusive Mr. Wesley* (2nd ed., Nashville, Tenn., 2003), 166-185.

37. Dallimore, *Whitefield*, 2:472. See also 2:101-113.

38. Kidd, *Whitefield*, 201-203, 245, 246.

39. Especially see Dallimore, *Whitefield*, 2:113.

spreading branches, like an old oak.'[40] As he passionately phrased it a week earlier, 'whenever you return, you will be as welcome as gold to a miser.'[41]

Their Ministries

It is widely acknowledged that Whitefield's major influence was through his unique preaching. Newton acknowledged this in his tribute. Of his preaching, Newton declared, 'Here I always thought him unequaled*, and I hardly expect to see his equal while I live.' He was right and others agree still. As one historian recently said, 'his robust ministry and compelling passionate proclamation of the necessity of a new birth made him the eighteenth century's most sensational preacher in Great Britain and America.'[42] Newton warned in his tribute, that it was folly to duplicate Whitefield's unique style, but they could learn from him. Many conscientious pastors, once they saw how Whitefield preached for a response, devoted themselves to make increased impact through their preaching too. 'He introduced a way of close and lively application to the conscience, for which I believe many of the most admired and eminent preachers now living, will not be ashamed, or unwilling to acknowledge themselves his debtors.'

Preaching was important for Newton and he was very active preaching in his church and on periodic tours, as well as publishing many of these Sermons.[43] However, preach-

---

40. *Letters to a Wife*, 9 May 1774, in *Works* 5:583.

41. *Letters to a Wife*, 30 April 1774, in *Works* 5:579.

42. Schlenther, 'Whitefield,' ODNB.

43. *Six Discourses (or Sermons) as Intended for the Pulpit* (1760); *Twenty Sermons Preached at Olney* (1767); *Fifty Sermons on the Messiah* (1786), as well as others printed individually.

ing was not what people valued most in him. He once commented about a pastoral friend who was a poor preacher but an influential writer. Then Newton paused to reflect how this applied to himself too. 'I rather reckoned upon doing more good by some of my other works [hymn-writer, preacher] than my letters ... but the Lord said, "You shall be most useful by *them*; and I learned to say, "Thy will be done! Use me as Thou pleasest, only *make* me useful.'[44] In the end, this is what happened. In the early 1770s Newton periodically sent a letter to be published in the small monthly *Gospel Magazine*. Often these were to no one in particular but were in the form of a pastoral letter giving advice. When he saw that these were well received by his readers, he wrote more. In 1774 he published these as a collection of letters. Unlike Whitefield, Newton did not reveal his identity in his published letters. Instead he used the pen names of Omicron and Vigil. But word did get out among his acquaintances and this increased his popularity. He published more individual letters and when the public desired more, he decided to publish a book of his private letters.

So he asked some of his correspondents to loan him the letters he had sent them. He then edited these so the recipients' identities would not be known. In 1780 he published these in a two-volume set of more than one hundred and fifty letters to twenty-four individuals. The title was *Cardiphonia or The Utterances of the Heart, in a Collection of Letters Written in the Course of a Real Correspondence, by Omicron*. As before, Newton used his pen name to hide his identity. But when *Cardiphonia* was reviewed in the *Gospel Magazine*, the publisher included Newton's portrait

44. Quoted in Gordon, *Wise Counsel*, 141.

on the magazine cover and in the table of contents, listed his name as the author. Now those outside his circle
of friends knew his identity. Consequently, he regularly received a steady stream of letters from appreciative
readers and enquirers from England, Scotland, Holland,
South Africa and America. *Cardiphonia* became very popular and is still being republished. As a result, Newton collected further letters to be published as a sequel after his
death.[45] Since then, others have collected additional letters and published them.[46] The most recent is *Wise Counsel:
John Newton's Letter to John Ryland Jr.* (2009).[47] The Christian
public valued Newton's transparency, humility and wise
counsel. As a result, Alexander Whyte the noted Scottish
preacher is accurate when he declared that, 'Newton's
most distinctive office in the great Evangelical Revival
was to be a writer of spiritual letters.'[48]

It is interesting that Marcus Loane in his separate biographies of Whitefield and Newton uses the same term to
describe them, though in different areas. He says, 'Whitefield was the evangelist *par excellence* of the Evangelical
Revival,' and Newton was 'the letter-writer *par excellence*
of the Evangelical Revival.'[49] Further he makes another

---

45. For these letters see *Works* 1:131-704, 2:1-255, 6:1-373.

46. For an up-to-date list of these see Tony Reinke, *Newton on the Christian Life* (Wheaton, Ill., 2015), 19, 20.

47. Gordon, *Wise Counsel*. This book is unique in that each of the eighty-three letters is placed in its historical setting and extensive notes have been added. Further, because most are from MSS, formerly unknown information is revealed.

48. Quoted in Gordon, *Wise Counsel*, 141.

49. Marcus Loane, *Oxford and the Evangelical Succession* (1950; Christian Focus Publications, Fearn, Ross-Shire, 2007), 46, 91.

observation how Newton differed from Whitefield. This time he modifies a comment made famous by Whitefield and afterwards by Wesley. Of Newton he says, 'He would not itinerate like Whitefield' but 'made the parish his world while others made the world their parish.'[50] It is true that Newton did not physically travel extensively, but he did through the mail.[51] As G.R. Balleine put it, 'He was the St. Francis de Sales of the Evangelical movement, the great spiritual director of souls through the post.'[52]

---

50. Loane, *Oxford and the Evangelical Succession*, 82.

51. See Grant Gordon, 'John Newton: A Study of a Pastoral Corre-spondent,' [unpublished] Th.M. Thesis (Princeton Theological Seminary, 1987).

52. G.R. Balleine, *A History of the Evangelical Party in the Church of England* (London, 1908), 107.

9

Newton's Final Tribute to Whitefield

When George Whitefield died suddenly 30 September 1770 in Newburyport, Mass., the shocking news spread rapidly. It was just eleven days later 11 October 1770 that Newton preached his tribute of Whitefield to his congregation in Olney. That would have been the first Sunday after the news reached that little village. In that evening tribute Newton spoke of Whitefield's zeal, faithfulness, and his unique impact on England and abroad, as well as on their little town.

As mentioned above, Newton ended his sermon with these words. 'He introduced a way of close and lively application to the conscience, for which I believe many of the most admired and eminent preachers now living, will not be ashamed, or unwilling to acknowledge themselves his debtors.' Though not stated, that included Newton who felt much indebted to Whitefield for modelling how to preach effectively. But that final line, though true, does not sound how a caring and sensitive pastor, such as Newton, would have ended his sermon to a grieving congregation. That might have been the end of his written sermon notes, recognising he had very little time to prepare it, but one wonders what he said extemporaneously at the end.

His cover letter to the copy of his sermon that he sent to Joshua Symonds is very revealing in two ways. First it shows that Newton was realistic about Whitefield. Though Newton greatly valued Whitefield, this did not mean he was blind to Whitefield's weaknesses. On one occasion when he mentioned some of Whitefield's flaws or limitations, Symonds misinterpreted Newton's comment.[1] Symonds wrongly assumed that Newton valued Wesley over Whitefield. Therefore, five days after Newton preached his tribute to Whitefield, he sent Symonds a copy of that sermon and explained his reasons for honouring the memory of Whitefield. 'Last Lord's-day evening, I preached to a very large auditory, on occasion of Mr. Whitefield's death. As you once so *greatly misunderstood* me, as to think that I was prejudiced against him, and even preferred Mr. Wesley to him, I have sent you what I wrote of my sermon [emphasis added].' 'You will thereby see,' he continues, 'what was my judgment of him, which has been my abiding judgment for many years. What I may have mentioned to you was not inconsistent with this; for had he not had his blemishes and mistakes as well as others, he would have been more than man.'[2]

Secondly, the letter reveals how Newton probably concluded that sermon as he finished his notes and spoke from his pastoral heart to his congregation. Newton mentioned to Symonds that the sermon notes he had sent him were

---

1. It is not known what Newton had said. Possibly it was the unwise claim made by Whitefield at his son's baptism, mentioned earlier. On one occasion to Polly, Newton described another minister as having 'Whitefield's excellence without any of his foibles' (quoted in Martin, *Whitefield*, 211).

2. Newton to Joshua Symonds, 16 Nov. 1770, ALS is MS 00263 (Emory Family Papers) in Fisher Rare Book Library, University of Toronto.

'(*as far as it goes*) ... *nearly verbatim* the same that I spoke from the pulpit (emphasis added).' So Newton did say more extemporaneously. As he expressed it to Symonds, 'he is now at rest: he is now with the Lord whom he loved. ... he is rejoicing.' One can hear these words flowing out over the large congregation that night. Probably some there had joined the crowd of 2,000, thirty-one years earlier, to hear the twenty-four-year-old Whitefield first preach to them in a field because their pastor at the time would not open his pulpit to this fiery preacher. And maybe too they were among those who begged him to come back two days later and stood in the heavy rain to hear him once more. Those two days in Olney would be typical of what Whitefield would experience during the rest of his life: rejection by many of the local clergy, preaching in the open air, and powerful revival results of people *hearing* and *feeling* and *convicted* of sin. Others in the congregation who were younger no doubt heard Whitefield on his subsequent visits to Olney. So that is why in 1770 Newton called the town's people together once more; this time to pay their tribute. As Newton expressed to Symonds, 'He was much beloved at Olney, and had been *a great blessing to me*. I, therefore, thought it incumbent on me to bear my public testimony to him [emphasis added].'[3] He expanded this later in his letter to Lord Dartmouth. 'I thought it expedient and even incumbent on me, to bear public testimony to his character as a minister, especially in this place, where he was known and dear to many and had been despised and misrepresented by many more.'[4]

---

3. Newton to Joshua Symonds, 16 Nov. 1770.

4. Newton to Dartmouth, 19 Jan. 1771, *Historical Manuscripts Commission ... Dartmouth*, 192.

He also admitted to Symonds that he had another motive for preaching that sermon. He continued, 'Besides, I expected (as it proved) that the occasion would bring many to church. The Lord was pleased to give me liberty; and I am not without hopes* it might be a useful opportunity.' That effort would have greatly pleased Whitefield who used every opportunity to draw people under the sound of the gospel. Now fifteen years after first encountering Whitefield, Newton was following the example of his model Calvinistic preacher-evangelist whom he much admired. Of Whitefield, Newton said to Polly, 'he warms my heart, makes me more indifferent to cares and crosses, and strengthens my faith.' [5] Now Newton sought to do the same for the many who gathered that evening in the little village of Olney.

---

5. *Letters to a Wife*, 12 Sept. 1755 in *Works*, 5: 502, 503.

Bibliography

Manuscripts

Bridwell Library, Special Collections, Perkins School of Theology, Southern Methodist University, Dallas, TX.

> Samuel Brewer to George Whitefield, 23 Aug. 1769. ‹http://digitalcollections.smu.edu/cdm/singleitem/collection/white/id/4/rec/12›[accessed 15 Jan 2014].

David M. Rubenstein Rare Book & Manuscript Library, Duke University.

> Newton to Mary (Polly), 19 Feb. 1767 (Frank Baker Collection; Newton Letters; Box CO 7).

> Whitefield to Mrs. Leighton, 14 Oct. 1762 (Frank Baker Collection; Mrs. Leighton's Letter Book; Box CO 5, Folder 7).

Dr. Williams Library, London.

> Newton to Jennings, MS #39.98(46-57). This library has thirteen MS letters of Newton to Jennings (6 July 1750 –26 Jan. 1760).

Firestone Library, Princeton University.

> John Newton diaries (22 Dec. 1751-5 June 1756) and (1 Jan. 1773-21 Mar. 1805), CO 199 (no. 1319) vol.1. Bound Manuscripts Collection. First Series. Manuscripts Division. Department of Rare Books and Special Collections. Princeton University Library.

Lambeth Palace, London.

> Newton to Polly (no date), MS 2935 (f. 218).

> Newton to Polly, 28 Dec. 1758, MS 2935 (f. 24).

> Newton to Whitefield, 2 Jan. 1756, MS 2935 (ff. 232, 233).

> Newton Journal MS 2937. This has now been transcribed by Marylynn Rouse and published by The John Newton Project, Stratford-upon-Avon as *Ministry on My Mind* (2008).

> Newton Diary for 1767. MS 2941. This is a pocket book in which he kept a 'brief account of the principal events that have occurred.'

Morgan Library and Museum, New York, N.Y.
> Newton diary (23 Sept. 1756- 31 Dec. 1773) MA 731.

Seattle Pacific University Library, Special Collections, Seattle, Wash.

> John Newton to John Campbell, 1 Aug., 1794, ‹http://digitalcommons.spu.edu/cgi/viewcontent.cgi?article=1028&context=newton_campbell›[accessed 26 July, 2015].

Thomas Fisher Rare Book Library, University of Toronto.

> Newton to Joshua Symonds, Nov, 16, 1770, ALS is MS 00263 (Emory Family Papers).

West Yorkshire Archive Service, West Yorkshire.

> Newton to Rev. Henry Crooke, of Leeds. MS Catalogue Ref CL.

Published Sources

Aitken, Jonathan, *John Newton: From Disgrace to Amazing Grace* (Wheaton, 2007).

Baker, Frank, 'Grimshaw, William (1708-1763)', *DEB*, 480-482.

Balleine, G. R., *A History of the Evangelical Party in the Church of England* (London, 1908).

Bull, Josiah, *Now I See: The Life of John Newton* (Edinburgh reprint, 1998). First published as *John Newton of Olney and St. Mary Woolnoth* (1868).

Bull, Josiah, ed. *Letters of John Newton with biographical sketches* (1869, Edinburgh reprint 2007).

Carter, Grayson, 'Dartmouth, Earl of (1731-1801)', *DEB*, 292, 293.

Cashin, Edward J. , *Beloved Bethesda: A History of George Whitefield's Home for Boys, 1740-2000* (Macon, GA, 2001).

Cecil, Richard, *Memoirs of the Rev. John Newton*, in *Works*, 1:vi-129.

Cecil, Richard; ed. Marylynn Rouse, *The Life of John Newton* (Christian Focus Publications, Fearn, Ross-shire, 2000).

Cheetham, J. Keith, *On the Trail of John Wesley* (Glasgow, 2003).

Clipson, E. F.,'Fawcett, John (1740-1817)', *DEB*, 381.

Clipson, E. F., 'Gifford, Andrew (1700-1784)', *DEB*, 438.

Collins, Kenneth J., 'Wesley's life and ministry' in Randy L. Maddox and Jason E. Vickers, eds., *The Cambridge Companion to John Wesley* (Cambridge, 2010), 43-59.

Cook, Faith, *William Grimshaw of Haworth* (Edinburgh, 1997).

Copson, S. L., 'Johnson, John (1705/6–1791)', *Oxford Dictionary of National Biography*, Oxford University Press, 2004 <http://www.oxforddnb.com/view/article/14894>[accessed 17 Jan 2014].

Coulter, Milton J., 'Whitefield, George (1714-1770)', *DEB*, 1180-1181.

Dallimore, Arnold, *George Whitefield: God's Anointed Servant in the Great Revival of the Eighteenth Century* (Westchester, Ill., 1990).

Dallimore, Arnold, *George Whitefield*, 2 vols. (Edinburgh; American Edition 1980).

Dawbarn, Robert, "The 'Johnsonian Baptists'," *Transactions of the Baptist Historical Society* 3.1 (May 1912): 54-61.

Demaray, Donald, *The Innovation of John Newton* (Lewiston, NY, 1988).

Elliott-Binns, L. E., *The Early Evangelicals* (1953, Cambridge reprint, 2002).

Erskine, Ralph, *Gospel Sonnets* (6th edn., London, 1755).

Ervine, W. J. Clyde, 'Venn, Henry (1724-1797)', *DEB*, 1137, 1138.

Gatiss, Lee, 'George Whitefield: The Anglican Evangelist,' *The Southern Baptist Journal of Theology* (Summer 2014), 71-81.

Gatiss, Lee, ed., *The Sermons of George Whitefield*, 2 vols. (Wheaton, Ill., 2012).

Gillies, John, ed., *The Works of the Reverend George Whitefield*, 6 vols. (London, 1771-1772).

Gillies, John, ed., *Memoirs of the Life of the Rev. George Whitefield* (London, 1772).

Gordon, Grant

'John Newton: A Study of a Pastoral Correspondent,' [unpublished] Th.M. thesis (Princeton Theological Seminary, 1987).

'A Revealing Unpublished Letter of George Whitefield to John Collett Ryland,' *Baptist Quarterly*, April 2016 [proposed date of issue].

Wise Counsel: The Letters of John Newton to John Ryland Jr. (Edinburgh, 2009).

Gore, John, *Gore's Liverpool Directory* (Liverpool, 1766).

Halyburton, Thomas, *Life and Death of Thomas Halyburton* (2nd edn., London, 1718).

Hayden, Roger, *Continuity and Change: Evangelical Calvinism among eighteenth-century Baptist Ministers Trained at Bristol Academy, 1690-1791* (Oxfordshire, 2006).

Haykin, Michael, A. G.

The British Particular Baptists 1638-1910, 3 vols., (Springfield, Mo., 1998-2003).

The Revived Puritan: The Spirituality of George Whitefield (Dundas, On, 2000).

Hayward, Samuel and Samuel Pike, *Some Important Cases of Conscience Answered, at the Casuistical Exercise, on Wednesday Evenings, in Little St. Helen's, Bishopsgate-Street.* (London, 1755).

Heitzenrater, Richard P., *The Elusive Mr. Wesley* (2nd edn., Nashville, Tenn., 2003).

Henry, Matthew, *The Communicants Companion* (14 edn., 1752).

Hervey, James, *Theron and Aspasio* (Edinburgh, 1755).

Hindmarsh, Bruce, *The English Conversion Narrative* (Oxford, 2005).

The Life and Spirituality of John Newton (Vancouver, B.C., 1998).

John Newton and the English Evangelical Tradition (Oxford, 1996).

'Newton, John (1725-1807)', *Oxford Dictionary of National Biography*, Oxford University Press, 2004 ‹http://www.oxforddnb.com/view/article/20062›[accessed 20 Jan 2014].

Historical Manuscripts Commission. XV report, Appendix, Part 1, The Manuscripts of the Earl of Dartmouth, vol. III (London, 1896).

Johnson, Samuel, *A Dictionary of the English Language* (London, 1768).

Johnston, E. A., *George Whitefield: A Definitive Biography*, 2 vols. (Stoke-on-Trent, 2008).

Kidd, Thomas S., *George Whitefield: America's Spiritual Founding Father* (New Haven, CT, 2014).

Klein, Milton, *An Amazing Grace: John Thornton and the Clapham Sect* (New Orleans, LA, 2004).

Lambert, Frank, *'Pedlar in Divinity': George Whitefield and the Transatlantic Revivals* (Princeton, 1994).

Lewis, D. M., ed., *Dictionary of Evangelical Biography, 1730–1860*, 2 vols. (Oxford, 1995; Peabody, Mass., reprint, 2004).

'Life of Rev. Samuel Brewer,' *Evangelical Magazine* (1797), 5-18.

Loane, Marcus, *Oxford and the Evangelical Succession* (1950; Christian Focus Publications, Fearn, Ross-Shire, 2007).

Maddox, Randy L. and Jason E. Vickers, eds., *The Cambridge Companion to John Wesley* (Cambridge, 2010).

M., J., 'History of the Baptist Church at Rawdon,' *Baptist Magazine* (1818), 10:458,459.

Mahaffey, Jerome Dean, *The Accidental Revolutionary: George Whitefield & the Creation of America* (Waco, TX, 2011), 15.

Martin, Bernard, *John Newton* (London, 1950).

McInerney, Vincent, ed., *Slaver Captain: John Newton* (Seaforth, 2010). This includes updated versions of *Authentic Narrative* and *Thoughts on the African Slave Trade* (Barnsley, 1788).

'Memoir of the Late Rev. J. Newton (part 2),' *The Evangelical Magazine* (1808), 97-112.

Methodist Heritage Handbook 2010 (Methodist Church House, London, 2010).

Milner, Joseph, *The History of the Church of Christ* (London, 1794 -1797).

Naylor, Peter, 'John Collett Ryland (1723-1792),' in Michael Haykin, ed., *The British Particular Baptists 1638-1910*, 3 vols. (Springfield, Mo., 1998-2003), 1:184-201.

Newton, John,

An *Authentic Narrative of Some Remarkable and Interesting Particulars in the Life of ***** Communicated in a Series of Letters to the Rev. Mr. Haweis, Rector of Aldwincle, Northamptonshire and by Him (at the request of Friends) Now Made Public* (London, 1764).

Apologia (1784) in *Works* 5:1-58.

Cardiphonia or The Utterances of the Heart, in a Collection of Letters Written in the Course of a Real Correspondence, by Omicron (1780) in *Works* 1:422-704, 2:3-255.

The Christian Correspondent; or a series of religious letters, written by John Newton ....to Alex. Clunie (Hull, 1790).

Letters and Conversational Remarks of the Rev. John Newton (London, 1808), ed. John Campbell.

Letters to a Wife in *Works* 5: 303-644.

Memoirs of the life of the late Rev. William Grimshaw ...In six letters to the Rev. Henry Foster (London, 1799).

Olney Hymns (1779) in *Works* 3:299-679.

One Hundred and Twenty Nine Letters from the Rev. John Newton to the Rev. William Bull (London, 1847), ed. Thomas P. Bull.

Review of Ecclesiastical History (1769) in *Works* 2:2-297.

Six Discourses (or Sermons), as Intended for the Pulpit (1760) in *Works* 2:256-354.

Thoughts Upon the African Slave Trade (London, 1788) in *Works* 6:519-549.

Twenty-five Letters of John Newton [to Jones] (Edinburgh, 1840).

The Works of John Newton, 6 vols. (1820, Edinburgh reprint, 1985).

Noll, Mark, *The Rise of Evangelicalism: The Age of Edwards, Whitefield and the Wesleys* (Downers Grove, Ill., 2003).

'The origin, names of ministers of a Particular Baptist Church now meeting in Byrom Street Liverpool,' *Baptist Magazine and Literary Review*, vol. 8 (1816), 498, 499.

Owen, John, *Christologia* (new edn., London, 1725).

Perry, Fred, *Travel with William Grimshaw* (Leominster, 2004).

Philip, Robert, *The Life and Times of George Whitefield* (1837; Edinburgh reprint, 2009).

Phipps, William E., *Amazing Grace in John Newton: Slave Ship Captain, Hymn Writer and Abolitionist* (Macon, GA, 2001).

Pollard, Arthur, 'Crook, Henry (1708-1770)', *DEB.* 271, 272.

Rack, Henry D., *Reasonable Enthusiast: John Wesley and the Rise of Methodism* (3rd ed., Peterborough, 2002).

Rawlin, Richard, *Christ the Righteousness of his People: or, The Doctrine of Justification by Faith in Him* (Glasgow, 1753).

Reinke, Tony, *Newton on the Christian Life* (Wheaton, Ill., 2015).

Rouse, Marylynn.

> *Life of John Newton* (1827) by Richard Cecil; edited and expanded by Marylynn Rouse (Christian Focus Publications, Fearn, Ross-shire, 2000).

> *Ministry on My Mind* (The John Newton Project, Stratford-upon-Avon, 2008).

> *The Searcher of Hearts* (Christian Focus Publications, Fearn, Ross-shire, 1997).

Ryland, John, ed., *The Work of Faith, the Labour of Love and the Patience of Hope: Illustrated in the Life and Death of Rev. Andrew Fuller* (2nd edn,. London, 1818).

Ryle, J.C., *Five Christian Leaders of the Eighteenth Century* (1868, Edinburgh reprint 1960).

Schlenther, Boyd Stanley, 'Whitefield, George (1714–1770)', *Oxford Dictionary of National Biography*, Oxford University Press, 2004; online edn., May 2010 <http://www.oxforddnb.com/view/article/29281 >[accessed 13 Dec 2013].

Schlenther, Boyd Stanley and Eryn Mant White, *Calendar of the Trevecka Letters* (Aberystwyth, Wales, 2003).

Seymour, A. C. H., *The Life and Times of Selina, Countess of Huntingdon*, 2 vols. (London, 1844).

Shenton, Tim,

>A Cornish Revival: The Life and Times of Samuel Walker of Truro (Darlington, 2002).

>An Iron Pillar: The Life and Times of William Romaine (Darlington, 2004).

Stout, Harry S., *The Divine Dramatist: George Whitefield and the Rise of Modern Evangelicalism* (Grand Rapids, Mich., 1991).

'Timeline of John Wesley,' Museum of Methodism, Wesley Chapel, London, ⟨http://www.wesleyschapel.org.uk/timeline.htm⟩ [accessed 20 Jan 2013].

Turner, Steve, *Amazing Grace* (New York, 2002).

Tyerman, Luke, *The Life of George Whitefield*, 2 vols. (New York, 1877).

Tyerman, Luke, *The Life of the Rev. John Wesley*, 2 vols. (3rd. ed., London, 1876).

Tyson, John R. with Boyd S. Schlenther, *In the Midst of Early Methodism: Lady Huntingdon and Her Correspondence* (Plymouth, UK, 2006).

Wallace, James, *A General and Descriptive History of the Ancient and Present State of the Town of Liverpool*, (Liverpool, 1795).

Ward, W. Reginald and Richard P. Heitzenrater, eds., *The Works of John Wesley* (Nashville, Tenn., 1991-2003).

Welch, Edwin, ed., *Two Calvinistic Methodist Chapels 1743-1811. The London Tabernacle and Spa Fields Chapel* (London, 1975).

Welch, Edwin, 'Andrew Kinsman's Churches at Plymouth,' *Report of the Transactions of the Devonshire Association for the*

Advancement of Science, Literature and Art, 97 (1965), 212-236.

Wesley, John, *Free Grace: A sermon preached at Bristol* (Bristol, 1739).

Whelan, Timothy D. , transcriber and ed., *Baptist Autographs in the John Rylands University Library of Manchester, 1741-1845* (Macon, Ga., 2009).

Whitefield, George,

    A Communion Morning's Companion (London, 1755).

    Hymns for Social Worship ... for Use of the Congregation in London (London, 1753).

    A letter to the Rev. Mr. John Wesley in Answer to his Sermon 'Free Grace' (London, 1741).

    Letters of George Whitefield, for the Period 1734-1742 (Edinburgh; Carlisle reprint 1976; reprint vol. 1 of *Whitefield's Works*, 1771, plus additional letters).

Wilberforce, Samuel, *The Life of William Wilberforce* (revised and condensed from original edition, London, 1768).

Wood, A. Skevington, *Thomas Haweis:1734-1820* (London, 1957).

Wright, Thomas, *Town of Cowper* (London, 1886).

Index

John Newton

Marylynne Rouse and Richard Cecil

Richard Cecil's classic biography of Newton is considered to be his 'authorised' biography as he both knew Newton well and allowed him to see most of the manuscript before publication. Marylynn Rouse has used the intervening years, and the wealth of information since made public, well by adding many other details and contemporary happenings to Newton's life story.

Some aspects of Newton's life are well-known: his involvement in the slave trade; his friendship with the poet William Cowper and the politician William Wilberforce; his gift as a hymn writer; his ministry, first in Olney, then in London.

But Marylynn Rouse has gone further and provides fascinating pieces of information regarding those who influenced Newton as well as those who were influenced by him. Here we see not only Newton the public figure, but we also see Newton in private, as a loving husband and father, as a concerned pastor and letter-writer.

ISBN 978-1-85792-284-4

George Whitefield: The Evangelist

JOHN POLLOCK

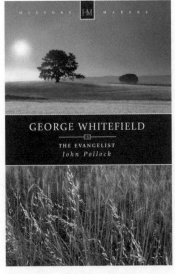

John Pollock vividly portrays George Whitefield and his times – George's long search for peace with God, his joy at being forgiven and justified through Christ's atoning death and then his enthusiastic sharing of the gospel. Often facing misunderstanding and even opposition from the established Church, he started to preach in the open air, beginning among the mining community and those who normally wouldn't come into Church. The story is told of how God worked in a remarkable way through George in Britain and also in the Colonies of America. Travelling many miles by horseback, crossing the Atlantic on countless occasions, sometimes experiencing illness and fatigue, countless people were drawn to Christ through this man – the 'Billy Graham' of his time. Come and catch the drama and also the passion and commitment George Whitefield had for the gospel.

ISBN 978-1-84550-454-0

Christian Focus Publications

Our mission statement –

STAYING FAITHFUL
In dependence upon God we seek to impact the world through literature faithful to His infallible Word, the Bible. Our aim is to ensure that the Lord Jesus Christ is presented as the only hope to obtain forgiveness of sin, live a useful life and look forward to heaven with Him.

Our books are published in four imprints:

CHRISTIAN
FOCUS

CHRISTIAN
HERITAGE

Popular works including biographies, commentaries, basic doctrine and Christian living.

Books representing some of the best material from the rich heritage of the church.

MENTOR

CF4•K

Books written at a level suitable for Bible College and seminary students, pastors, and other serious readers. The imprint includes commentaries, doctrinal studies, examination of current issues and church history.

Children's books for quality Bible teaching and for all age groups: Sunday school curriculum, puzzle and activity books; personal and family devotional titles, biographies and inspirational stories – because you are never too young to know Jesus!

Christian Focus Publications Ltd,
Geanies House, Fearn, Ross-shire,
IV20 1TW, Scotland, United Kingdom.
www.christianfocus.com